Europe's
Green
Alternative

Europe's Green Alternative

Penny Kemp
Carlos Antunes
Pierre Juquin
Isabelle Stengers
Wilfrid Telkamper
Frieder Otto Wolf

Translated by Julia Sallabank

GREEN
PRINT

First published in 1992 by
Green Print
an imprint of The Merlin Press
10 Malden Road, London NW5 3HR

ISBN 1 85425 050 7

Phototypeset by Computerset Ltd, Harmondsworth, Middlesex,
England

Printed in Canada

Contents

4 Joint action 92

Appendices

Glossary 113

In this book the term *billion* is used to mean one thousand million.

Land areas are given in hectares. 100 hectares equal 1 square kilometre. To help the reader make meaningful comparisons, it may be useful to know that the areas of certain countries are as follows:

Australia   768 million hectares
Belgium   3 million hectares
Canada   997 million hectares
Eire   7 million hectares
England   13 million hectares
France   55 million hectares
Scotland   7.8 million hectares
USA   936 million hectares
Wales   2 million hectares

Preface

The idea for this book began in April 1989 when Pierre Juquin and Frieder Otto Wolf met with Carlos Antunes in Lisbon. They had gathered to celebrate the anniversary of the 'Carnation Revolution', and demand the release of Otelo de Carvalho and his companions. During their stay, they talked of the need for a new direction for Europe. After many hours of discussion, they agreed to look for like-minded Europeans who would attempt to produce a manifesto which embraced the new concept of eco-socialism.

A two-day meeting was arranged in Cologne where the circle was widened and discussions began in earnest. At times, it seemed an impossible task as differences in emphasis and style had to be overcome, but eventually the book began to take shape. A few weeks later, we all met again in Paris and the subsequent text is the fruit of our combined labours.

Since the completion of the book the need for a new way of looking at the world has become urgent. As I write this, over 27 million people are suffering malnutrition in Africa, over a hundred thousand children are threatened with death in Iraq, child prostitution in Latin America has doubled and the gap between the world's rich and poor has increased significantly. A better understanding of our environment has given us the knowledge to realise just how urgent the ecological crisis is.

Meanwhile Europe is changing rapidly. Momentous events starting with the Polish Solidarity movement, and continuing with Soviet perestroika, have caused upheaval in central and eastern Europe. The effects of these events will no doubt be felt for some time to come; they will have more and more repercussions on life and our way of looking at it. We now know the effects of pollution, we have all heard of the greenhouse effect and the hole in the ozone layer, and politicians from all countries are making 'green' noises. However, missing from the political agenda is a determination to question the existing political structures and systems under which we live and work. All those people who abhor the moves by leaders such as Bush and Major who are already talking in terms of their new world orders must be prepared to actively work towards a truly just and sustainable world.

This manifesto is but a prelude, an overture to an adventure which is in its infancy. It is being published in most European languages and contributions for future editions have been offered from eastern writers. We do not claim to have all the answers, indeed we would be foolish to pretend that we do. We hope that this work will make a contribution to the dialogue that is at present affecting all of us, whether we live in Europe or beyond, as we now realise that the ecological crisis that we face is not confined to individual nation states. We know that Europe can play a leading role in halting the injustice and inhumanity in this world and that all it takes is political will. We sincerely hope that this dialogue will lead to an East/West conference in Berlin. Early preparations have started. Our dearest wish is for our work to be superseded by new dialogue – in each country and between countries – clearing the way for a green, eco-socialist alternative.

Penny Kemp
June 1991

Introduction

Politicians of all colours are busily trying to emulate the greens' early success. However, the green movement in Western and Central Europe, and also in the Soviet Union and elsewhere, is but one of the momentous upheavals underlining the crisis in orthodox politics – the widening split between traditional ways of treating problems, and the problems themselves. Ecological questions are among the issues in the changes currently taking place in the countries of Eastern Europe.

The movement is only just beginning. We now know that life on earth is not immortal, and that its death would not be a natural death, but a man-made one. Now that the realisation has been made, it would be irresponsible of humanity not to change its ways as quickly and as totally as it can. No society will be able to evade the need for change, but orthodox politics has made no preparations to meet this challenge. The traditional parties think they have an answer to everything, but now their fount of wisdom is dry.

The causes of the ecological and social crisis are not simple. Very different issues may be raised in East and West. Other factors will appear, in combinations as yet unknown to us. Current events in the East show how little can be foreseen. It is possible, but by no means certain, that a finer, more open, pluralist civilisation will emerge. On the other hand, the immense inequalities between one human being and another may lead to the best-prepared, best-organised and best-armed state, clan or class working out and imposing their own solutions based on oppression and exploitation, to the exclusion of poor people, women and some of the young. They may dress the century's wounds, but they will not treat the whole ailment. They will change just enough for the system to continue unaltered.

But the professional politicians who claim to have the situation under control are lying, and the number of people who realise this is growing. Thus, real progress for humanity is possible, as long as we are able to think and act in unison and not leave the steering to established power and wealth. The gravity of the problem is such that we consider it time for a public debate to be started on possible solutions for the benefit of all humanity, including future generations. We are starting the ball rolling with a few concrete proposals. Of course, a project to change the course of history cannot be contained in one word. We are simply making our position clear at the beginning of the debate. We have all been involved in left-wing politics for some time, on paths which have sometimes converged, and sometimes diverged. We stand for the solution we see as the best in Europe: an eco-socialist alternative — feminist, pacifist and anti-authoritarian.

In this manifesto, we are laying out our main collective ideas and intentions. We are submitting them to general view, whilst remaining aware of the limits of our current research, and of the imperative need for a profound, honest dialogue with all those who are wondering what the outcome will be, whatever route they have followed. We are willing to listen to anybody, especially young people. This book is being published in several languages, and afterwards we will publish the first responses, whether approving, improving or disapproving.

There are no ready-made solutions, in the West or in the East. Before we choose, we must investigate all the options fully. But choose we must.

PART
ONE

The challenges

In London in 1848, Karl Marx wrote in *The Communist Manifesto:* 'Although the bourgeoisie has scarcely been in power for a century, it has created more massive and more colossal forces of production than all the past generations put together. Subjection of nature's forces to man, mechanisation, application of chemistry to industry and agriculture, steamships, railways, electric telegraphy, clearing of whole continents for cultivation, canalisation of rivers, whole populations conjured out of the ground; what previous century would have suspected that such forces of production lay dormant in the bosom of society?'

Five or six generations have passed since these words were written, the mere batting of an eyelid in comparison with the two million years that have passed since the human race appeared. In France, for example, a worker had to work for 1 hour and 43 minutes to buy a loaf of bread in 1875, compared to 10 minutes today; 1 hour 26 minutes for a litre of milk compared to 7 minutes today; 4 hours 46 minutes for a litre of petrol compared to 10 minutes now. At the same time, the legal length of the working week has shrunk from 63 hours to 39. Average life expectancy in France had risen from 28 years in 1780 to 44 years a century later; today we can expect to live to over 80. Refrigerators, washing machines, television sets and cars feature abundantly, if not quite equally, in most homes in western Europe. But what does this way of life really mean for people?

New facts and new problems have emerged: ecological considerations, women's liberation, the liberation of the peoples of Africa, Asia, Latin America and Oceania, and alienation from work, society and politics in the heart of the 'rich' countries. The model of civilisation invented by the bourgeoisie is being questioned. There is a new momentum to the demand for the abolition of the capitalist mode of production. But socialism is also being questioned, with an unexpected forcefulness; socialism, that is, in the form in which it has manifested itself up till now, in complicity with the bourgeois model of civilisation – albeit with its own specific characteristics. In calling the working-class movement to transcend this model, socialism risks being superseded itself.

Ecology, society and economics

Ever since life first emerged on Earth, it has been constantly evolving, transforming its surroundings as it does so. Human beings have had to adapt to changes in climate and react to natural phenomena, even quite recently as in the mini ice age from the mid-sixteenth century to the mid-nineteenth.

However, the problem is now reversed: it is the human race which is changing nature. Apart from pollution and the depletion of natural resources, we are capable of provoking cataclysms of the order of volcanic eruptions and earthquakes, or worse. We have begun to decimate animal and plant species, and to disrupt food chains. We have put poisons into the ecosystem which will remain there for thousands of years. We are changing the chemical composition of the atmosphere. At our most extreme, we are capable of a war which would cause a nuclear winter, killing off all higher life forms on Earth almost instantaneously.

Never in the history of the world have such wide-ranging changes been wrought in so short a time. By the speed and scale of these changes our relationship with nature is also changing. Nature itself is not in danger; it will continue, no matter what. It is the shape of life on Earth, and first and foremost human life, which is now in the balance. This is the main consequence of capitalism. Up till now, socialism has been incapable of arresting this mis-development. On the contrary, it has produced the same effects in a shorter period of time. The evidence is right before our eyes.

Planet in peril

The chemical composition of the atmosphere began to change in the second half of the nineteenth century. Since then, the burning of coal, oil and wood has freed more carbon dioxide than can be absorbed by the oceans and by photosynthesis. The gap has widened more quickly since the early 1950s, however. Nature took five thousand years, at the end of the last ice age, to increase the level of carbon dioxide by 50 per cent. At the present rate, human society will have doubled this level in under a hundred years – a hundred times more quickly. Since the mid-1980s, other gases emitted by human activity – methane, nitrogen and chlorine compounds – have doubled the greenhouse effect caused by the carbon dioxide. All these changes cannot avoid altering the climate. Ozone is, at most, only a 3mm-thick layer between us and the sun, the third of a millionth of the depth of the atmosphere. But these 3mm, by filtering out the sun's ultraviolet rays before they reach the ground, have allowed life to develop on Earth. Even the slightest change in the effectiveness of this filter could have incalculable effects for living cells and for photosynthesis. The stability of ozone depends on a multitude of physical and chemical interactions. In the last few years, certain industrial products which make up less than one hundred millionth of the total – the infamous CFCs – have been sufficient to undermine its stability.

In a few thousand years, humanity has transformed vast areas into deserts or semi-deserts. This destruction is accelerating. Every 20 seconds, a cultivable field disappears somewhere on the planet. The burden of chemicals carried by the environment and by living things in general is growing at an alarming rate (not just due to agricultural practices, but also to medicine). In Europe, and also more generally in the industrialised countries of the northern hemisphere, forests are dying. Acid rain is only one of the factors. An increase of 1 per cent per year in road transport in the EC would lead to 80,000 extra tonnes of oxides being released each year; after one or two decades no forest would remain. Eastern Germany, Poland and Czechoslovakia make large contributions to the destruction with their emissions of pollutants. Each year, in what is left of the tropical rain forest, an area nearly the equivalent of West Germany is cut down or burnt.

Two-thirds of the global population lack clean drinking water. Every day 25,000 people die from this. Dirty water kills 4.6 million children a year. In several industrialised countries, groundwater has been polluted. At the present rate, in ten years' time two-thirds of the flow of all the world's rivers will be checked by huge dams, with catastrophic consequences. In spite of their vastness, the oceans of the world will soon no longer be able to digest the 20 million tonnes of rubbish that humans throw into them every year, nor cope with the oil spills. This is murder – but also slow suicide. Other problems are appearing, for instance pollution by ever-shorter electromagnetic waves, used massively in technical applications.

Each ecological phenomenon is a secret to be unfurled. Discovering more about our ecology can also act as a truth serum, as the answers shed a new, critical light on the dominant system of production and consumption. Many people are finding that it is shaking them out of ways of thinking which have been, until now, like prisons.

Earn your living – lose your life?

At the same time, the exploitation of millions of people, men and women, continues. It results from the sordid capitalist tendency to treat human beings as factory fodder to be bought and sold like any other merchandise. In this system, the relationship between employers and employees is not essentially a human relationship, but an economic one. Millions of people are only allowed to live in exchange for their productive work. These women and men are forced to sell an essential part of their vital activity to a third party in order to procure the means for survival. Work becomes a means of existence, not a way of freely developing their personality.

This dependency exists, whatever the price offered for the work. Nevertheless, the system does tend to keep the price within certain limits determined by profit margins. On the one hand, it is aiming for ever-increasing production with a corresponding requirement for more workers; on the other hand, however, it keeps a constant supply of workers in reserve (either by technical innovation or by lay-offs) so as to divide and rule them by keeping them in competition rather than in solidarity. Unemployment, insecurity, undervaluing women's work, decreasing incomes from small and medium-sized farms, over-exploitation of the Third World (either by immigration or directly in Asia, Africa, Latin America or Oceania), vast areas of poverty even in the richest countries: these are not accidental by-products of the system, but in-built characteristics.

Dependency, however, goes well beyond this formal act of subjugation. Neither the wage system nor competition, important as they are, define sufficiently the economic dominance of capitalism. It emanates from the very process of production that capitalism has instituted: 'Masses of workers, crammed into factories, are organised along military lines. The foot soldiers of industry, they are placed under the surveillance of a whole hierarchy of officers. They are not only the slaves of the bourgeois class and state, but every day, every hour, they are the slaves of the machine, the foreman, and above all of the bourgeois factory owner himself' (*Communist Manifesto*). As Marx points out in an 'unpublished chapter' of *Das Kapital*, 'it is a specialised mode of production, not only with regard to technology, but with regard to the real conditions of the work process. This is the capitalist method of production. It is only now that the real subordination of work to capital can be seen'.

Technology and mechanisation are no more neutral towards human beings than they are towards ecosystems. In all capitalist production methods, conditions of work (in the widest sense) dominate the worker, instead of being under his or her control. 'The means of working, turned into an automaton, towers above the worker during the very work process, in the shape of capitalism which overpowers and pumps out his life force' (*Das Kapital*, II, p. 105). It is catastrophic that the experience of communism in Eastern Europe maintained this real subjugation, by duplicating in its planned economies the capitalist methods of production which exploit nature so intensively and reduce the worker to the rank of machine, or cog. For two centuries workers have been struggling. They have opposed divisive competitiveness with solidarity, obtained reductions in the working week, fought for better conditions. But they have not managed to overcome their real subjugation. In the United States and the European capitalist states, they have just lost the first stages of the battle of modernisation.

In fact, not content with using up human and technical resources, capitalism is hard at work altering structures and putting in place a new system of attaining growth, which will ensure the continued subordination of human beings to production methods. The aim is to shorten the life of the means of production, transferring them rapidly from one part of the globe to another: in short, to make production itself the main product. Automation, processing factories, and the re-allocation of tasks will not in themselves put an end to the subordination of the human being to the machine, to the technical division of labour into parcels of tasks, nor to the multiplication of unskilled, or at any rate non-intellectual, tasks. A supervisory job is not necessarily an intellectual one. These innovations introduce new divisions and fragment the workforce, particularly with the tendency to detach the least qualified jobs and give them to sub-contractors, temporary staff, or casual workers (young people especially). Computerisation is introducing previously exempt professions to machine-subordination, particularly in service industries. What is more, capitalism is increasing the dependency of the whole population by creating needs which can only be satisfied by the purchase of more merchandise. Here too, in different political and social structures and inferior levels of technology and production, the countries of Eastern Europe have to face up to similar challenges.

Capitalism and ecology

It would be simplistic to reduce the whole world economy to capitalism. There are other fundamental aspects of exploitation, such as patriarchy. There are also other modes of production. However, it can be seen that capitalist modes of production have constituted the main part of the world economy for several centuries, that capitalist logic underlies the structure of the majority of modern nation-states and social classes, and that capitalism is still the dominant force in development, imposing its model on Eastern European countries and invading Africa, Asia, Latin America and Oceania.

Who was responsible for the oil slick from the *Amoco Cadiz*? Standard Oil of New Jersey. And for the one in Alaska? Exxon. Who refuses to recognise new rules forbidding the dumping of oil at sea? The 'flags of convenience', i.e. the immense merchant fleets under the command of industrial and financial groupings. Who caused the chemical disaster at Seveso? Hoffman-Laroche. The one in Basle? Sandoz. Who caused the one in Bhopal, India? Union Carbide, whose worldwide profits that year shot up by 304 per cent. Who produces and consumes over half of all the weedkiller produced in the world? The United States. Who produces and consumes half of all fungicides? The EC. Who is pressurising the peasants of Africa, Asia, and Latin America to do the same? Giant billboards advertise the pesticides of Bayer, Hoechst and Schering in the paddy-fields of the Philippines. Although it is banned in their own countries, the chemical producers of the industrialised world continue to produce DDT, and sell it to peasants in other continents. Business is good. Over the last four years, the Dutch multinational Unilever (with 291,000 employees and over 500 subsidiaries in 75 countries) has increased its net profits by a billion florins. Half of its business is in food products (Astra, Lipton, Royco, Iglo etc.) and half in specialised chemical products (fertilisers, detergents, toiletries). It aims for 4 per cent growth per year by imposing its model of consumption on Japan and south-east Asia. Annual profits from world production of CFCs, the ozone killers, amount to $3 billion, or at least $50 billion if you include all the industrial applications. Three-quarters of the production is concentrated in five countries: seven US multi-nationals, with Dupont of Nemours at the top of the list (35 per cent); Autochem in France; Hoechst in West Germany; ICI in the United Kingdom . . . with subsidiaries in Spain, Italy and Greece. Consumption of these products is growing in Africa, Asia and Latin America, but only 5 per cent of the total is produced there.

Who is behind Amazonian deforestation? Twenty US mul-tinationals, among them Union Carbide, Massey Ferguson, Chrysler, Ford and Bethlem Steel; ten Japanese multina-tionals, including Mitsubishi, Toshiba, Sony, Suzuki; six West German multinationals, for example Volkswagen and Bosch; five Italian multinationals (Ferrari, Fiat, Pirelli . . .); three British multinationals; and the Swiss group Nestlé. The mineral riches from the Grande Carajas project have already been divided up, three hundred years in advance, between Japanese, US and Western European multinationals. Every-where in Asia, Africa and Latin America, the World Bank and the International Monetary Fund are at the centre of enter-prises which violate nature and human beings. 60 per cent of the world's remaining tropical forests are situated in five of the most indebted countries: Brazil, Indonesia, Zaïre, Peru and Colombia.

These are the social forces which, a hundred and fifty years ago in Europe, threw women and children into mines and factories for up to eighteen hours a day, and crammed families into insalubrious tenements. It is they who today, in the northern hemisphere, are closing and relocating enterprises, making millions of people redundant and dictating how they live. It is they who, in South Africa, subject black people to Apartheid, they who extract immense profits from the work of their former slaves, immigrants, workers, peasants and Third World seamen. They who, in Amazonia, are inflicting a 'final solution' on the Indians, who make the exploited *favellas* work for less than a hundred dollars a month, outlaw trade unions and load the pistols which killed Chico Mendes.

As for the 'socialist' countries: we will subject them to the scrutiny they deserve later – not just a historical scrutiny, but one which serves as a warning for all of us. Private profit does not explain everything.

Responsibility

In our eyes it is obvious that structures play a fundamental role in societies. They shape people's lives. To a large extent, they determine mentality, ideas, opinions, behaviour. This begs the question of how much freedom we really have, and what possibility we have of curbing, halting and reversing the systems and changing the structures.

Each person in Europe bears some responsibility. In Great Britain, a family of four produces 44 tonnes of carbon dioxide per year: 25 per cent from the family car and 3 per cent from public transport. One car consumes as much oxygen in 1000 kilometres as a human being breathes in a whole year. Washing a car uses, on average, 190 litres of water. A washing machine uses 120 litres with each load. A dishwasher uses 80 litres. Of course, most people have no choice – the system forces them to act like this. But responsibility is not without its social differences: in Paris, in the more expensive *quartiers*, each inhabitant uses over 200 litres of water a day, whereas in the poorer districts each person uses only 90 litres. But we still all bear responsibility. We melt tropical forests in our cups of coffee and hot chocolate, and crunch them in our hamburgers. DDT and other dangerous pesticides are sold to Burkina Faso so that we can buy green beans in February. In Germany, the price of a cup of Guatemalan coffee can be broken down as follows: 14 per cent for the German supermarket, 5 per cent for the packaging and transport industries, 12 per cent for the mechanical and automobile industries, 5 per cent for the chemical industry, 1 per cent for the importer, over 30 per cent to the West German government in taxes and duties, 3 per cent for the Guatemalan land owner, 7.5 per cent to the Guatemalan government in export duties, and 4 per cent for the peasant who produced the coffee. Stress, snobbery and advertising: consumption of coffee in Western Germany has increased tenfold since the 1950s.

We all share the true responsibility, individually and collectively. We ought to unite against the system, not compromise ourselves by putting up with it. If we follow the logic of ecology to its end, we will see that contrary to what classical economic theories tell us, capitalism is not inescapable, and that it would have been possible to go down other paths to development in the modern era. But ecology does not harbour any illusions than any other economic system based on productivism would resolve the problems. Ecology draws its strength from its criticism of all those economic theories that were conceived in the nineteenth century without taking into account either the ecosystem or demography.

Neo-liberalism? 'Environmental policies'?

Luckily, capitalism is currently incapable of imposing a kind of 'eco-fascist' dictatorship, and is therefore wavering between the scenarios.

First, there is the neo-liberal scenario. But watch out! For centuries, the 'invisible hand' of the market, of which Adam Smith spoke, has been at work. What makes us think that our customary selfishness towards each other and nature is going to disappear overnight? How are our competing choices going to combine in harmony with the ecosystem and happiness for all? As productivity is currently defined as the return on each employee, without taking into account social and ecological costs, the mechanisms for increasing productivity would continue to create production techniques which would only further aggravate unemployment, work-related stress and the violence inflicted on nature. Capitalism is continually intervening, by means of the very visible hand of the banks, multinationals and the state, to preserve the conditions for its well-being and its profits. This is what Ronald Reagan and

Margaret Thatcher proved in practice, and what we see in 'liberal' Japan or the newly-industrialised countries of Asia.

A number of capitalists prefer another method of defending their interests. In the 1930s and 1940s, a social compromise, the Keynesian compromise, was introduced in the United States. After the Second World War, this 'American way of life' spread to other capitalist countries. However, this compromise, the result of long conflicts and marked by social contradictions, has now exhausted its possibilities – or reached its limits. For the moment, there does not seem to be any other social compromise emerging which is favourable to employees and consumers. Should we therefore look towards adapting it to ecological requirements?

In an often-quoted passage from *Das Kapital*, Marx writes: 'Capitalism simultaneously exhausts the two sources of all riches: the earth and the worker'. As capitalism has evolved, it has put into place safeguards to conserve the workforce and ensure its maintenance. Today, analogous solutions could be put into place to safeguard nature. To state the alternatives as either the rapid destruction of capitalism or suicide for humanity is simplistic. Ecological reform of capitalism is already under way in the northern hemisphere, under the banner of 'ecological policies': these include controls on private and public enterprises, penal or financial sanctions for crimes against the environment, and research into techniques of limiting ecological damage whilst opening up new possibilities for accumulating capital (e.g. impact studies to reduce costs, recycling to produce extra resources, the invention of new products to attract new consumers, the sale of non-polluting, low-energy equipment, etc).

Such ecological advances do conflict with some of the interests of capitalism and the state, but they are taking place in several countries. Assuming that the 'invisible hand' does not nip them in the bud, an eco-Keynesian compromise would be for ecology what increased standards of living or social security are for socialism: real progress, yes, but limited, provisory, and contradictory.

Such environmental policies put forward a scenario where private property will remain in control of the means of production, the market, competition, and the freedom to speculate: in other words, the essential factors for free-for-all growth, *laisser-faire*, and the absence of controls on technology and the economy. They can therefore only ever be a partial measure, carried out here and there, mitigating rather than preventing the damage.

Environmental policies exist within the framework of the present economic accounting system. It is inevitable that they will come up against the virtual impossibility of translating ecological costs and risks into monetary terms in advance. Those involved in the politics of health know this problem already.

Environmental policies depend on the state apparatus and on the will of financial and industrial groups, and can even reinforce these interests. On the ground, they cannot have the subtlety, the precision, or the radical approach of direct democratic intervention.

If only it were still possible to say: 'Let's deal with the most urgent thing first. We'll solve the ecological problems at once. Once we've preserved the basic conditions for human life, then we can get down to the social problems.' But the poor people of the rich countries, and the multitudes in Africa, Asia, Latin America and Oceania, cannot wait. Is a solution to the ecological crisis credible if it does not tackle social problems? In short, we do not think that the answer is to search for new ways to continue capitalist production, but to resolve all our human and ecological problems as effectively as possible.

Two logics

There are two opposing logics: on the one side, economics divorced from all other considerations; and on the other, life and society.

As a series of exchanges between societies and nature, the economy has constituted the material basis for all human life and reproduction for the last two million years. But capitalism turned the economy into a closed, domineering system, isolated from nature. In just a few centuries, economics overwhelmed societies by stating that human needs are unlimited, and that nature has an unlimited capacity to fulfil them. This meant reducing everything to its immediate usefulness. The vast field of everything which could not be measured or translated into terms of immediate economic gain was regarded as luxury, superfluous, laziness or utopian – unless it could be marketed. From this point of view, ecosystems are only inert worlds to be pillaged and poisoned at will. Human beings are defined by their capacity to work and consume, transformed from free subjects into objects.

Such postulations explain why capitalism has such a tendency to expand and replicate itself. The planet is becoming one enormous shopping centre, where billboards announce, with characteristic arrogance towards the poor: 'If you don't know what you want, come in! We've got it!'

Capitalism is always trying to mould people into its own mutilated, economic image of how individuals should be. It glorifies a blinkered ideal of happiness. It forces everyone into a gasping rat-race, channelled in the direction of profit. The determining factor is the exchange value of money – practical values have second place. At the very extreme, capitalism's ideal products are arms and drugs, which provide the maximum profits for the minimum tying up of assets. The economy as a closed system, but nature and humanity as infinitely exploitable: a double contradiction.

The economy has never operated as a sealed vessel. All living beings and all societies depend on energy, and can only replace what they have used by drawing fresh energy from their environment. Energy cannot be created by human effort. It comes ultimately from the sun, either directly (as light or heat), indirectly (as in wind or water power), or from radiated heat stored in fossil fuels (oil, coal, gas), with a small proportion (on a planetary scale) now coming from geothermic flux (heat pumps) and nuclear energy.

In modern industrial economies, abiotic sources of energy have largely supplanted not only human labour, but also the majority of organic energy sources. In these economies, human labour represents, in general, less than 1 per cent of the total mechanical force utilised. Economic activity draws its raw materials from nature, then throws them back. This activity itself squanders energy. To extract a tonne of copper from porphyritic deposits with a 1 per cent concentration of metal ore requires 22,500 kilowatt-hours; the cost rises to 43,000 kilowatt-hours for a concentration of only 0.5 per cent, or to 90,000 kilowatt-hours for a 0.3 per cent concentration. To extract one tonne from sea water, it is thought that 560,000 kilowatt-hours would be needed.

By increased mechanisation, the use of chemicals, and the sophisticated processing of harvested produce, agriculture is becoming a mining activity. It is substituting energy from oil for increased acreage, or in other words, fossil energy for solar energy. Its efficiency is thus falling in real terms. In 1963, Great Britain already used 6.5 fossil fuel calories for each calorie of food produced; in 1970, the United States' ratio was 9.6 to 1.

If all the 6 billion people in the world were to use as much energy per head as is used in the United States, energy demand would immediately be increased tenfold. In less than a hundred years, with population levels staying constant, all coal reserves (even unproven ones) would be exhausted. Oil supplies would run out in eighteen months. The atmosphere would probably not survive. Given the current level of technological knowledge, only the construction of nuclear fast breeder reactors could satisfy such a demand in theory. But how many Chernobyls would there be on a planet crammed with nuclear reactors? What effects, known or still unknown, would the 'normal' levels of radiation have? What would we do with the waste, which in the case of plutonium 239 (half-life 24,600 years) would have to be dealt with by beings as far removed from ourselves as we are from cave men?

Human beings cannot be divided and compressed at will. Modern anthropology is finding that perhaps ever since we evolved, we have possessed characteristics which prevent us from being reduced to mere working machines. These characteristics include our ability to devote ourselves to useful work, probably much wider in scope, more subtle and more diverse than the simple stone tools that have been found would imply: it also includes the reproduction of the species, which is much more than sex and our attempts at education and upbringing. Language, too, was certainly not born solely from economic requirements, but from the need to communicate over the whole gamut of human relations. Our capacity for pleasure, in work as well as in play, in love and in conviviality, and in our artistic creativeness, which appeared very early; and last but not least, human dignity, expressed in the most ancient times by the respect afforded to the dead.

Itself a product of industrialisation, part of the working class never ceased to ponder these fundamental questions. In 1848-50 they fought mechanisation and its dehumanising isolation. In the 1930s, they fought Taylorism. More and more, nowadays, workers are demanding more than just a job and a wage. They are asking the question, 'What are we producing? Why, for whom, and how are we producing it?'

The deeper they probe, the more conscious they become of the purpose of production. At the same time as other movements of which they have as yet scarcely heard, the new workers' movements are moving towards the fulfilment of the age-old aspiration: 'to each according to their needs'. But they are also starting to think about the needs themselves. The realisation of the whole individual is a central part of their aims.

A new radicalism

There is still a long path to tread before the economy is relegated to its proper place in society and in relation to nature, and before economic freedom is redefined as a person's freedom for self-determination as a worker and a consumer in the act of production, and as the freedom to produce by consciously inserting human actions into natural cycles. This new radicalism, both ecological and humanitarian, highlights economism's double blind spot: the rationality it only applies to the short term, switching it off with regard to long-term consequences. It leads society astray by breaking down problems into questions so specialised that they only tackle one aspect, thus preventing us from thinking globally.

Previously, societies were able to expand outwards. This is no longer possible. Between ten and twelve thousand years ago, this planet had about five million inhabitants. There are now over five billion humans. According to low estimates, there will be ten billion in a century's time. Even if we do succeed in reducing the birth rate sufficiently, will we be able to refuse to improve life expectancy in all countries, and so increase the total number of people? There is nothing catastrophic in this realty, so long as production, needs and consumption are structured along radical new lines that are *just* and *ecological*.

There is no escape route. There are no more Americas to be conquered. Constructing a new planet, or emigrating to the star Alpha Centauri, are pseudo-scientific dreams which just avoid the real structural problems. The present system cannot be extended to the whole planet. If all humanity were to be fed using the agricultural techniques current in the United States, all the world's oil reserves would be used up in 50 years on agriculture alone, and soil and water would suffer irredeemable damage. In the United States, there is one car for every

1.8 inhabitants, whereas the world average is one car for 12 people. If the level of car-owning in the United States were common throughout the world, there would immediately be three billion cars, and double that within a century. It is unthinkable.

Society will only find a way out of this mess by abandoning present patterns of production and consumption. From now on, any historical compromise will have to take social and ecological factors into account. Seldom has the hackneyed word 'breakthrough' had such a clear meaning. By combining ecosystems with human societies, we believe that we can find the eco-socialist path that Europe needs. Let us try to reconcile the two sets of demands and timescales into a practical synthesis to create new, ecologically sustainable ways of producing, consuming and living: an emancipated society.

Let's not act like prophets. There is no 'one best way'. We cannot ignore or re-write history. We do not want to manipulate people. The general problem, as we have outlined it, is not exactly the same in every European country. For example, there are considerable differences between the countries of the East and the West. A world we can all share can only be built from precise solutions tailored to the individual problems, but all with the same aim. In this manifesto, we are limiting ourselves to suggesting solutions adequate for the problems of the countries in which we live. But at the same time we are proposing to debate the problems and solutions with any social and political group from the Eastern countries who are interested in an alternative. We want exchange, co-operation, and mutual help, without any kind of domination.

There need be no apocalypse. There would be no ecological problem if humanity had not organised itself into societies as soon as it emerged and started to substitute culture and history for biological evolution. One characteristic which developed from our intelligence, and from our choice not to follow the path of the survival of the fittest, is solidarity. The human species holds in its very character the source both of the current tragedy, and of the possible way out.

The answer to the challenges will not come from unconscious forces such as nature or economics. It can only come from concerted, conscious action. It will not be technical, but cultural, or *political* in the true sense. The solution does not lie in a Malthusian denial of human abilities and needs. This kind of fundamentalist approach, sometimes referred to as 'deep ecology', would solve the problem of production by getting rid of production, and solve the problem of humanity's relationship with nature by getting rid of the humans. No; for us, eco-socialism can only be humanitarian. Together, let us increase our intelligence and our solidarity – in other words, our humanity.

2

Women's liberation

Socialism, ecology, feminism: these currents were not born from the same contradictions. Even if all ecologists became feminists, and all feminists ecologists, the two movements would still be distinct.

Feminism is basically about fighting domination.

It is true that women are biologically linked to the reproduction of the human species. But it does not follow that they therefore have an essential affinity with nature. The 'macho' view of women as 'natural' beings on the one hand, and men as 'cultural' beings on the other, is ridiculous. The roles of both sexes are determined by our culture. The dominance of social relationships by men for thousands of years, and the division of roles in bourgeois society, have produced femininity and masculinity as we know them. Women are no closer to nature than men. The women's liberation movement and the ecology movement grew up simultaneously, the first even more widespread than the second. Both have in common the way they question the whole system from an outside point of view. Because their experience is different to men's, women can make different contributions to society.

Patriarchy excludes women from political, economic and military power, limiting them to looking after the children while subjecting them to mutilation and frustration. Women develop interpersonal skills which men have cut themselves off from in favour of hierarchical, competitive ways of behaving. Women have fought, and are still fighting, for control of their own bodies. They know better than men what damage can be caused by the social pressure that leads to the denial of one or the other of the component parts of a personality. Since entering the modern workplace, women have had to juggle work, children, housework, and a whole range of other activities. They are in a position to see paid employment in its true proportion to the rest of their life, whereas for many men it still constitutes their main way of measuring their identity.

In Asia, Africa, Latin America and Oceania, women bear the full brunt of industrial over-exploitation and the unplanned growth of sprawling shanty-towns. They bear and feed the children, and flee before famine and violence. They carry out all the chores necessary for survival: in rural areas, tens of thousands every day trudge miles for inaccessible drinking water or to collect thirty or forty kilos of firewood or food plants, which are becoming so scarce that they take up to a day's walk to reach. And everywhere in the world, they are resisting the economic and ecological crimes which are also crimes against women. For example, in the Indian Himalayas the women's non-violent 'Chipko' movement made the loggers turn back by hugging the trees. In Kenya in 1984, there were 637,000 women registered as members of 16,232 women's groups; today the groups number over 25,000. In Peru, a local women's self-help movement, 'Vital', now has 1500 communal kitchens in the slums of Lima. And there are other examples in Indonesia, Bangladesh, the Philippines, Sri Lanka, Zimbabwe, Brazil, Mexico . . .

Feminism and work

Who has prepared our food and drink for the last few thousand years? Who washes, irons and mends the clothes? Who does the housework? Who looks after the children? Without these activities being undertaken every day, no society or economy would remain on its feet. According to the United Nations, women worldwide do two-thirds of all the hours worked, produce 44 per cent of all foodstuffs, receive 10 per cent of the world's wages and own 1 per cent of the property.

But the classical, phallocratic school of political economics invented by men denies the existence of domestic productivity, and only sees the family as a consuming unit. Apparently, the home neither produces, nor adds value to merchandise. But the woman who changes a nappy, prepares meals, and brings up her children, is engaged in work of immense practical value. As well as being their workplace, for many women the family and home is the place where alienation, and often also violence, are at their worst. Whilst women's work represents the same number of hours as paid work, national accounting ignores it. By only attaching value to paid work, for the last two hundred years capitalism has succeeded in keeping domestic work under its control. Women are the ones who maintain the workforce. By buying the workforce, capitalism exploits women's unpaid work, whether or not they have a paid job too. Capitalism has only been able to develop thanks to the patriarchal model which burdens women with an enormous quantity of unvalued work, which is seen as a 'natural' function and not as work at all. Domestic work, denied and unpaid, sets the pattern for women's conditions of employment.

Despite gradual changes, women have to make their own way in a men's world. Nearly all find that the whole concept and organisation of work is along masculine lines. Men still see paid work for women as only a short digression in their lives; their place is in the service of their partner and family. Women are still in second place in society. In industry they have been put in a subordinate position, as a reserve in case of economic difficulties, subjected to Taylorism and to inequalities of pay, qualifications and responsibilities. This is truly dual economy.

We are fighting for equality for women and men in paid work. But when the ecological and economic crisis betrays the deficiencies in the patriarchal values of utilitarianism, technocracy and the unbridled exploitation of resources, it is important to continue to tackle the basics. In the European labour movement, the approach to paid work has by and large remained a masculine one. Laws, agreements and conventions abound with special dispositions and rights accorded to women. But many of these measures tend to restrict them still further into their maternal role. The whole basis of work has to be re-thought, for both sexes. Only if we challenge women's oppression can we open the way to the end of all exploitation.

The body

Sexuality is a social construct. The same behaviour that treats nature as a passive, inexhaustible object sees the reproduction of human life not as a free, creative activity by women, but as a resource to be exploited by men at will. 'Masters and owners' of women's wombs as well as of nature, men have taken more and more control over women's fertility, and thus over their sexuality, their health, and their lives.

In many countries, women have chosen to fight first for their own bodies.

Every situation is different, from one country to another, and from one woman to another. Not all women are beaten, not all have been raped or forced into prostitution, not all have endured unwanted pregnancies five to seven times in under ten years. But every time a woman speaks out about these daily tragedies, the circle of solitude, silence and suffering is broken, uniting women in their experience of male violence and domination. The most intimate of problems is also the most political. Women's bodies, controlled by male society and still so frequently manipulated, harassed, incarcerated and mutilated, reveal the monstrous nature of this society. From this comes the essential demand: 'A child if I want, when I want'. Laws have been fought for and won, though macho interests still seek to question or overturn them. Each unwanted pregnancy is a battleground – it is the woman who should decide. As long as contraception, which must itself be contrllled by women, is not absolutely certain, the voluntary termination of pregnancy must assure women's freedom of choice.

Planet-wide, the average number of children per woman is 3.5. In the Third World it is 4.1. In ten countries, the average is over 7: these include Saudi Arabia, Jordan, Syria, Libya, Benin, Nigeria, and Kenya. In fifty others, the birth rate is over 5.5 per woman.

In 1974, at the world population conference held in Bucharest, the response of many states, foremost of which was Algeria, to proposals for population control was: 'the best contraceptive is development'. There is truth in this. But yet again, economic factors have taken first place. How many economists pretend to believe that a rise in GNP is sufficient to bring the birth rate down! In fact, the richest countries are not always those with the lowest birth rates, and the poorest do not always have the highest rate of population growth. Should we condone state terrorism? According to some, states should force women to limit the number of children they have. This is the way China chose to try to get to the bottom of the population growth table. The repression of Tien An Men Square shows what patriarchal despotism can cost. The Chinese leadership now estimates the cost of the degradation of the environment in their country at 15 per cent of national revenue, and that a major ecological crisis is possible there in the next twenty years. Are they going to add ecological dictatorship to their demographic dictatorship? We reject these devastating methods anywhere.

The issues are complex. First and foremost, we are against campaigns designed to distract. Whether by witch trials or by the use of modern technology, it is the same panic impulses in people that the authoritarian, patriarchal, imperialist forces are trying to manipulate.

These forces, which forbade and punished abortion in Europe for centuries, are now trying to use ecological arguments to justify repressive policies to control women in Africa, Asia and Latin America. We say that population management depends on women's liberation. Once taboos are broken and barriers overthrown by a sufficiently large number of women, as soon as women are not so confined to the role of procreators and keepers of male-headed households, the fall in the birth rate is often rapid. How many pioneering women have paid the high price of breaking with tradition: loneliness, isolation, exclusion.

Legal and technical measures are needed such as the promotion of women's education, the fixing of a minimum legal age for marriage, the legalisation of contraception, encouraging women to go out to work. The state should take responsibility for these, and should not impose or favour one particular model or norm of sexuality. The decisive factor remains that population levels fall when the status of women rises.

The great monotheistic religions cannot escape from this debate. They are confronted by real changes among their faithful.

In Roman Catholic northern Italy, the birth rate is among the lowest in the world. In Ireland, the average number of children per woman has sunk from four to two in the last twenty years. The same changes are taking place in Spain. In Brazil, Mexico, and Colombia, the condemnation of contraception is being challenged both by some theologians and by the real drop in birth rates in the last two decades.

Throughout the Islamic world, from Bangladesh to Morocco, birth rates are already falling: in Tunisia, Morocco and Turkey, in the central Asian Soviet Republics, even in Egypt and Algeria (which decided in 1979 to 'actively promote birth control'). In May 1971 in Tunis, the Congress of Moslem Women demanded the end of polygamy and the respect of female dignity, basing their demands on the Koran. In nu-

merous Islamic countries, the sale and advertising of con-
traceptives are legal, and abortion has been liberalised.

Let us add – and we shall return to this theme – that while
supporting women's control over their own bodies, we wish to
express our mistrust of techniques for manipulating reproduction and our opposition to the genetic manipulation of human
beings.

Questioning power

All this is not exclusively the responsibility of women. It is
important that women create a feminist consciousness, in the
same way as the labour movement once tried to create a class
consciousness. However, the feminist movement calls upon
everyone to become a feminist, men as much as women.
Feminism is one of the chances we have to found a new kind of
politics. Politics has everything to gain from becoming less
sophisticated, less artificial, closer to everyday life and, in
consequence, more human at heart.

The women's movement has widened the boundaries of
politics by placing its main emphasis on problems previously
relegated to private life. It has created its own independent
political structure. Established politics has tried hard to confine this creativity to a ghetto. Building one's own little patch
of freedom against and on the margins of the dominant culture
is not a good basis from which to transform the whole of
society.

Feminism has tried to infiltrate our institutions – but
politics has remained masculine. Men are accustomed to
looking at reality through a veil – the veil of power. In society's
institutions, women are in a minority; men dominate them not
just by numbers, but also by their customs and ways of
speaking. Women leaders have appeared. However, their posi-
tions have often made them women in name only, contributing to and reproducing the dominant structures and
stereotypes.

Male violence has compelled women to seek protection
from the state. The state is not, however, sexually neuter. Its
repressive measures profit the anti-feminist status quo. This is
the tangle of contradictions in which the women's liberation
movement has had to evolve. Should it work within the state,
and risk being swallowed up? Flee outside and risk losing one

of the means available to it? The question is how to work out strategies which make use of the state's apparatus, while preventing the movement from being subsumed and its objectives turned on their heads.

Women are already teaching men how to become more aware in their politics: by listening to each other, taking other people's points of view into account, and being sensitive to domestic constraints, childcare needs etc. But the existing political structures can digest and exploit these feminine capacities. Whether they want to or not, women as individuals or in a minority can only serve to perpetuate structures designed to perpetuate power. Women's only chance to enter politics and change it, without being destroyed or absorbed, is to enter *en masse*.

We are fighting for equal numbers of men and women in all levels of politics. We are aware of the limited nature of this demand, and of the need to push further for change. But it certainly goes further than the slogan, 'More women in politics!' Equal numbers would create the base from which women could start to transform political structures and ways of thinking. This would not be without problems for men – loss of power, conflicting interests – which would in turn lead to deeper questions being debated and resolved. As eco-socialists, we would like all European countries not only to adopt the principle of proportional representation in elections, but also to make it obligatory for each party to rotate candidatures between men and women. For men, feminism is not a matter of course. Like democracy, it has to be learnt. The change should bring a few surprises.

Eco-socialism must be feminist, or it will not succeed.

3

Towards dialogue between cultures

Since the time of the great cathedral builders, Europe has considered itself synonymous with Western civilisation. For five hundred years it has been the centre of the capitalist world. It has exported its wares, its soldiers and its missionaries to Africa, Asia, Latin America and Oceania. The societies in which we live are built on the syphoning-off of vast riches, and on the destruction of the peoples, cultures and ecosystems of five continents.

Less than a century ago, Britain, France and Germany were fighting for the title of most powerful nation on Earth. Now, the time when Europe was the world is over and European states no longer dominate the globe. Europe's child, the United States, has taken over, and cathedrals have given way to skyscrapers. Since 1890, the United States has been the richest country in the world. Today, part of Europe challenges the US on the world market, but is still dependent on its power, its technology, its ideas and its images.

Since 1868, Japan, the only non-European great economic power never to have been colonised by the West, has adapted Western techniques to take second or third place in the world's economic ranks. At the beginning of the 1980s, Japanese firms planted branches in a handful of newly-industrialised countries in Eastern and South-East Asia. Nowadays, over 40 per cent of direct Japanese investment goes to the United States, and about 30 per cent to the European members of the Organisation for Economic Cooperation and Development (OECD). The rapid economic expansion of this part of the world may be one of the characteristic phenomena of the twenty-first century.

The Soviet Union and the other countries who were members of COMECON have embarked on a number of wide-ranging transformations, whose outcome is still undecided.

But our picture of the planet would look very different if the wealth of each country corresponded to the number of its inhabitants.

Never so much wealth, never so much poverty

The two superpowers only contain approximately a twentieth of the world's population each. Three out of every five human beings live in Asia. China and India together hold 38 per cent of the planet's inhabitants. In three or four generations' time, one person in four will probably be African.

Two hundred years ago, the productivity of what is now the Third World was three times that of what are today the industrialised nations. A century ago, the scores were level, and now the Third World produces only a quarter of the goods the West does, although its population is much higher. In the eighteenth century, the gap between the productivity of farms in the two areas was only in the ratio of 1:2. In the nineteenth century, it was 1:10. Now a gap of 1:100 separates the Malian peasant farmer and a farmer in the United States.

Before the neolithic revolution, it is likely that no person earned more than one-and-a-half times as much as any other. The birth of agriculture probably widened the gap by a third in a few thousand years. After about two centuries of capitalism, the average GNP of the ten countries considered to be the poorest in the world (Ethiopia, Bangladesh, Burkina Faso, Mali, Bhutan, Mozambique, Nepal, Malawi, Zaire and Burma) corresponds to a hundredth of that of the rich, industrialised countries. A very well-to-do family in the United States has at its disposal an income 100,000 times larger than that of a poor family in one of the most destitute countries.

In 1986, the 500 major multinational companies could be divided up by parent country as follows: United States, 216; EC, 140; Japan, 87; other countries, 57. The 200 largest private multinational companies together have a turnover equivalent to a quarter of the annual production of the whole world. Only about fifteen countries have a domestic product which exceeds the turnover of the largest multinational in the world, General Motors. A few dozen countries produce less in value than the turnover of the 25 next largest companies. These multinationals control 90 per cent of all pineapple exports and forestry products; 85-90 per cent of wheat, coffee, maize, cotton, tobacco, and jute; 85 per cent of all cocoa; 80 per cent of tea, 70-75 per cent of bananas and natural rubber; 70 per cent of rice; and 60 per cent of sugar.

The West possesses three-quarters of the world's railway lines, an incomparable road network, an empire of shipping fleets, and all the main airline routes apart from ones to Eastern Europe. In France alone (550,000 sq km) there are 200,000 bridges. The United States alone controls 75 per cent of the world's television programmes, 89 per cent of computerised commercial information, and 65 per cent of commercial advertising. 88 per cent of all scientific articles are published in English. 400 journals (0.8 per cent of the total) review half of all publications.

The developed capitalist countries are responsible for between 75 and 80 per cent of all exports of manufactured products, and over two-thirds of all imports of raw materials. The bulk of trade in products manufactured by the developed capitalist nations is with each other. Trade in manufactured products between countries of the Third World ('South-South') represents only 30 per cent of their exports and 16 per cent of their imports. In fact, the developed capitalist countries export more raw materials than the Third World. Trade between former Eastern bloc countries and the South is low. 26 per cent of the world's population consumes 86 per cent of non-ferrous metals, 85 per cent of all paper, 80 per cent of the world's energy, 79 per cent of all steel, 53 per cent of edible fats, 38 per cent of proteins, and 34 per cent of the world's calories. The other three-quarters of humanity get what is left.

Today there are more people suffering from hunger than ever before. In 1980, there were 14 per cent more people without the maximum number of calories needed than in 1970. This is a complex, fluctuating world, and surveys vary in their pronouncements. The terms 'North, 'South', 'East', and 'Third World' do not reflect reality, however one misrepresents it. But there is nothing more real than inequality – and it is getting worse. Since 1974, after the 'oil crisis', five, then seven countries set themselves up as leaders of the world's economy: the United States, Japan, Germany, France, Britain, Italy, and Canada. Among its members, the EC unites all the colonial powers of 1914 except Russia.

Neo-colonial dominance takes on many forms. The international military, controlled by the nuclear club, has planted some 3000 bases on foreign soil. Military expenditure is far higher than the combined disposable income of all the two billion people living in China, India and Indonesia put together. The United States and the Soviet Union spend half of the total – that is over a million dollars a minute. In 1985, just the salaries and pensions of US army personnel came to over twenty times the GNP of Ethiopia. In half a day, the world spends enough on arms to finance the whole of the World Health Organisation's programme to fight malaria. Every eighteen to twenty months, the arms race indirectly kills as many people in Asia, Africa, Latin America and Oceania as died worldwide in the Second World War, by contributing to malnutrition, illness and illiteracy.

Industrialised countries from the East as well as from the West began to force-feed the Third World with arms in the 1950s. Today, 90 per cent of arms exports are from the industrialised nations, and 80 per cent of arms imports are into Third World countries. The three largest sellers are the United States, the Soviet Union and France. Britain is trying to build up its sales again. Germany is less and less willing to abide by the restrictions which still bind it. Italy, Spain, Greece and the Benelux countries are trying to corner parts of the market. It is only recently that the new, free Czechoslovakia has taken steps in the opposite direction. The armies and police forces of many Third World states are more often used against their under-fed compatriots than against foreign aggressors.

The great powers are in control of space, and of a large proportion of the oceans. If France was limited to its own territory, it would rank forty-fifth in the world in terms of the area of sea under its control. However, due to the number of colonies which it still keeps hold of, it occupies third place after the United States and Britain.

The great powers control international trade and tariffs. 107 out of the 500 largest banks are Japanese, 94 are North American, 190 Western European. In 1979, the amount of money bought and sold on stock exchanges was six times the value of world trade. In 1986 it was twenty times. The 'crash' of October 1987 wiped out $2000 million – twice the value of all Third World debt, and the equivalent of a whole year's world trade – an enormous, over-inflated speculative bubble. When world interest rates rise by 1 per cent, African debt rises by $1.5 billion. Banks and states have pressurised Third World countries to such an extent that they now finance the richest countries with their repayments. Export monoculture, over-stretched infrastructures, low wages and agricultural prices: these standard strategies dictated by the IMF and World Bank have shattered societies and ecosystems. In Morocco, levels of wheat production per inhabitant have fallen by over a half in thirty years to just below their 1930 level; formerly an exporter of cereals, Morocco now imports four-fifths of its needs.

These monetary and financial manoeuvres have cancelled out the rise in oil prices. In seven years (1980-87), the purchasing power of raw materials in relation to manufactured products fell by a third, so that it is back at its 1930 level. The miners of Bolivia are dying of misery caused by the prices set by London businessmen.

Capitalism is forcing a new division of labour on to the world. Internationalising production nowadays consists of accelerating the integration of production in the richest economies, where economic conditions are fairly homogenous. No large enterprise considers itself to be truly world-class if it does not have a foot in at least two zones of the 'triad' of the United States, EC, and Japan. The triad is itself currently undergoing internal readjustments.

In 1965, manufactured products only accounted for 18 per cent of exports from the Third World. By 1986, the proportion had risen to 41 per cent. The wealthy countries are still the specialists in industrial products, but mainly in semi-finished and chemical products, and products of the mechanical and electrical industries. Manufacture of traditional consumer products is being transferred to certain Third World countries, particularly those with 'free trade zones', where a million people, mainly women aged 16 to 25, are employed at low rates of pay on the assembly lines. Thus, six countries export 80 per cent of all Third World-manufactured products: Taiwan, South Korea, Hong Kong, Singapore, Brazil and Mexico. Eight countries – four in Latin America, four in Asia – receive as much in investments as 110 other Third World states put together. Six of them – Brazil, Mexico, Algeria, Venezuela, South Korea and Argentina – have received two-thirds of all the credit extended by private banks.

Asia, Africa, Latin America and part of Oceania lack energy, because the systems used by the capitalist countries (and Eastern Europe) are so wasteful, unfair and destructive. In order to avoid dependence on Southern oil producers, capitalist countries (like the United Kingdom) have not only exploited their own reserves, but have also launched into nuclear power programmes in defiance of the ecological risks.

While preserving its zones of influence in Latin America and the Pacific, capitalism has cut its mining investments in black Africa to one-tenth of former levels, and concentrated its efforts on its 'mineral belt' of Canada, Australia, South Africa and the Scandinavian countries. Without a care for the loss of factories and jobs in the northern hemisphere, or even whole regions, new materials have been substituted for raw materials imported from the Third World, finished products have been miniaturised, and new production and recycling processes have been introduced. Beneficial as these measures may be in some cases, they are not inspired by ecology or by new technology, but by imperialism alone. An increasing and correspondingly high level of waste products are being sent to the Third World.

Among West European states, French neo-colonialism is the most marked. France has kept some colonies. The size of its nuclear power programme (whose capacity increased sevenfold between 1975 and 1981) is unmatched anywhere. It also brandishes its own nuclear deterrent. A quarter of the uranium used in these comes from South Africa. In 1962, an expeditionary force was created specifically aimed at the Third World. French troops are deployed in Corsica, Senegal, Ivory Coast, Gabon, Djibouti, in the Central African Republic, in the Antilles, in Guyana, and in the Pacific. In 25 African countries, a network of agreements and hidden links, the 'franc zone' and the common tie of the French language all contribute towards the replacement of the empire by influence. This neo-colonialism maintains outdated economic, social and ecological systems.

An unsustainable world

The world created between the fifteenth and the twentieth centuries is not sustainable.

The still-dominant neo-liberal viewpoint cites the recent growth of some Asian countries as exemplary, and attributes their success to respect for the laws of the market. Not only does this view disregard the widely differing realities in Third World countries which mean that it cannot be applied universally, but, above all, it contradicts the very experiences which it cites in its own defence. The development of the Asian 'dragons' is due to a large extent to state control on a massive scale. All that remains of the neo-liberal theory is, on the one hand, brutal repression which blocks all attempts to form trade unions and protects the employers' absolute discretion; and on the other hand, insertion into the international division of labour brought about by the rich countries.

The IMF and the World Bank have no interest in upsetting the imbalance of trade between North and South. In fact, they try to maintain it by shifting its emphasis towards trade in goods with added value, and maintaining unequal levels of technology. South Korea, Taiwan, Singapore and Brazil are now trying to reject this polarisation of international specialisation – but financial restrictions hold them to it.

The Keynesian scenario, which was criticised in the Brandt report, and which the EC makes use of in its agreements with African, Caribbean and Pacific (ACP) nations, gives assurances that it takes into account the idea of a new world economic order. It is founded on the hypothesis that the economies of the North and South have mutual interests. It advocates stable, reasonable prices for raw materials and the transfer of large sums of money to the Third World, in exchange for the opening up of a large new market for the products of the rich countries. This model has had its day.

The prices of raw materials cannot stabilise in real terms, firstly because since 1900 they have had a structural, in-built tendency to fall, and secondly because exchange rates are too unstable. Apart from a few exceptions, in Third World petroleum-producing countries the rise in price of this basic product has not led to productive development but to a client economy which often benefits only a few monopoly-holders. The Keynesian analysis does not try to change the international division of labour. As specialisation in primary goods is not very profitable, Third World countries can only invest by becoming more dependent on finance from rich countries. The injection of capital is never enough to trigger off rational economic development, however. Its most common effect is merely to spread Western modes of production and consumption, encouraging wider inequalities and the destruction of ecosystems. The North only wins in the short term – the South does not win at all.

The extreme right's solution is to institute worldwide

apartheid. Like the old Roman Empire, Europe would surround itself with a 'wall' to keep out immigrants. It would relocate polluting industries, exploit the raw materials and agricultural produce of the Third World, and treat it as a dustbin. This solution could even lead to a parcelling-up of the world under the joint 'ownership' of East and West. However, Europe would only escape from the trap of the Cold War by entering into a war against the South. Like it or not, Europeans depend on the South. If Germany suddenly cuts its imports of ten 'strategic' mineral substances by 30 per cent, its own production would fall by up to 28 per cent in the short term.

Before the First World War, Lenin condemned the distribution of 'crumbs' stolen from the colonies to workers in the cities. Ecology teaches us that these crumbs are poison to all peoples. There will not be any island of green in a sea of pollution. In any case, the whole of Europe will only represent 3-6 per cent of the Earth's population in a hundred years' time.

The alternative solution

Europeans must change their way of thinking about politics, and remember that theirs is not the only culture. They must give up their claims to speak for the whole world, and start a dialogue about common values. The European model of development is approaching the point of ecological breakdown, whilst at the same time admitting that it is incapable of meeting the simple needs of several billion people. It cannot be reproduced in the Third World. Europe has not been able to break out of its mould, and now the mould itself is cracking up. It is those who question the basic mould of European life who stand a chance of changing it.

Europe prides itself on its 'civilising mission'. How many times has it betrayed its own values and trampled on human rights? The only source of riches apart from nature, the fount all riches, is human beings. Every *homo sapiens* is totally human, by our biology, by our ability to invent and learn, our capacity for abstract thought, and our sense of dignity and solidarity. If there are no frontiers for pollution, neither are there any frontiers for grey matter. It is not only capitalism, merchandise and speculation which spread throughout the world, but also people and ideas.

In order to create a new civilisation, all the different cultures on this planet need to speak to each other. Tens of millions of people in the Third World have already begun to think and experiment. For example, village communities in Latin America, Asia and Africa are organising their own development with the help of experts from the North and, increasingly, from the South. In Brazil, the Green Party, the Labour Party and the rubber-tappers' union are doing the same. Non-governmental organisations are emerging.

Humanity is an indivisible whole. But it cannot fulfil its potential by following just one model. The way forward is in a multitude of ecological and social patterns, in a planet with numerous cultures rather than one planetary culture – a 'pluriversal' planet.

This transformation will be difficult and presupposes that, on the one hand, Europeans will concentrate on solving their own problems using their own means. European eco-socialists are ready to take their part in this constructive responsibility. On the other hand, it presupposes that Europeans will refuse any solution that simply reconfirms their present privileges. As eco-socialists, we do not consider ecology to be a luxury for the wealthy. Our own standard of living is no more important to us than survival in the Third World. The problems, and the solutions, of North and South are interdependent.

Europeans must change their own modes of production, consumption and living, whilst ensuring that the Third World gains more autonomy. Europe must cancel the debts of Third World nations, and start new aid programmes whose sole aim is to redirect resources towards rural areas and food production, and to promote self-sufficiency in food. The countries of the Third World need to stop being confined to the role of just providers of raw materials and/or sub-contractors for multinationals because of capitalist and statistical advantages. The current pattern of specialisation must be replaced with a global, dynamic concept led from within Third World countries. This presupposes that exchanges between countries of the South will be encouraged, and that a Southern Bank will be formed.

We are not here to give examples or models to follow. Quite simply, we are, and will always be, on the side of the poor, the exploited, the outsiders and the downtrodden. 'Pluriversality' only makes sense if the world it invents is for them and with them.

4

Towards a new political culture

From Palestine to West Berlin, from Mexico to Moscow, from Gdansk to Amazonia or to Beijing, millions of people and innumerable groups, well-known or anonymous, are trying to take control of their own lives and write their own history. They are all part of a wave that is very slowly rising, a ripple of which appeared in 1968. Despite resistance, counter-currents, confusion and steps backwards, this movement is gradually eroding away all authority: employers, technocracy, patriarchy, the military, political parties, the church, the state. Affecting daily life as well as, if not more than, 'big decisions', the change is profound. The end of dictatorship in Greece, Spain and Portugal is all part of it, as were the struggles for democracy in Argentina, the Philippines and Chile, with all the problems of learning anew and growing pains that they bring. So also are the new social movements such as the 'grass-roots commissions' in Italy, the 'co-ordinations' in France, and the 'citizens' initiatives' in Germany – despite their limited agendas, their short duration, and their horror of (or difficulty in organising) stable structures.

May 1968 was the time of both the student rebellions in the West, and the Prague Spring. After that, *Solidarnosc*, together with movements in Hungary, East Germany, Czechoslovakia, Bulgaria, and the Soviet Union – who were sometimes still in a minority – demanded openness and complete democratic control of social processes by those affected by them. This is what the students in China also wanted. In these movements, young people play a prominent part. The European peace movement; anti-racist and immigrant movements such as that of second-generation North Africans in France; movements towards self-determination in Ireland, Wales, the Basque country, Corsica and others; new movements of peasants and farmers; lesbian and gay rights movements . . . in Western Europe, all these are to a greater or

lesser extent questioning the logic of power. So is the movement of non-governmental organisations towards solidarity
with the South. So, above all, is feminism. Without doubt,
other social movements will arise.

At the moment, in Western Europe, it is the green movement which, despite its contradictions, is giving the clearest
political expression to this groundswell. In Eastern Europe it
has taken on other forms, not totally defined, where ecological
concerns are nevertheless present. As eco-socialists we see this
general movement, in all its diversity, as a movement away
from alienation. A great gap separates the 'existence' of the
masses from their 'essence'. Their lives are inhuman when
compared to the view of humanity which can be drawn from
anthropology and other sciences, and the values drawn from
all humanity's most daring struggles, reflections and dreams
throughout history. All our large contemporary political organisations – liberal, socialist or communist – impose productivity at the expense of liberty, equality and ecology. They
treat the citizens of their countries as only marginal particip-
ants in the activities by which their needs are defined and
satisfied. From this springs the desire of an increasing number
to change the conditions of their lives.

In this sense, Marx was right when he pointed to the dual
nature of the working class: alienated, yes, but also yearning
for freedom. However, the difference is that today many
people are reacting to alienation in other fields apart from paid
work. We need to look more closely. Is it by chance that the
social composition of the new movements shows a large proportion of intellectuals and students? Is it a coincidence that
many workers are trying to change the quality of their life, not
only in the sphere of work, but also in the non-working areas of
their lives where they feel alienated? Some of the changes
currently taking place in the manufacturing and service industries are introducing the concept of individuals who are gener-
alists, but also free agents. Deep down, these are still all ways
of dominating and frustrating us as individuals and groups,
which an increasing number of women and men are refusing to
accept. These men and women want to take action, not have
their actions decided for them. Many of them have no abstract
notion of their growing alienation. This is the most common
course in history: they are taking concrete steps towards a new
world before working out a theoretical awareness of what they

are doing. A de-alienated society can only come from a real movement, not from the minds of theoreticians.

Let the state wither away . . .

The current situation is characterised by the contradiction between the growing power of most states (by means of the concentration of economic power, the extension of the areas in which the state intervenes, increased military might, police powers and computerisation), and the questioning of the state itself. This is inextricably linked with the extremes of state power which European societies have experienced in the twentieth century. The dual tendency which we have observed in the Soviet Union – questioning the power of the state (or, more exactly, of the party-state) over society and individuals, while attempting to solve the problems by the creation of a different type of strong state – is without doubt an illustration of the crucial debate which concerns all European societies.

Despite social movements seeking forms of self-management, the predominant model in both East and West today is still the liberal or social-democratic one. There is hardly any practical difference between the liberal and the Keynesian view of the role of the state. The liberals' fight against state control is an ideological disguise: in practice, they use the state to conduct their economic war, and thus a war against nature. Modern Keynesians are often close to the liberals in practice, and would like the rules of this double war to be stricter, but they raise no objections to continuing it, and can do little to lessen its scandalous effects.

In political circles – and even sometimes among the green parties – the idea is gaining ground that great collective emergencies such as the ecological crisis mean that the withering away of the state can be postponed indefinitely. Powerful state mechanisms, it is argued, are needed at all levels to manage the economy in the interest of preserving the eco-systems. Some people are already proclaiming the need for a world super-state.

This pushes the idea of a unified, centralised, hierarchical model of development to its very extreme. It perpetuates old authoritarian ideas, exemplified by the notion (belied by the facts) that state control is the best remedy for the capitalist disorder. The desire of states to regiment everything has been a large contributor to our present problems, in East and West. The state machinery is driven by the need to exercise power, and becomes further and further removed from real problems and their solutions. This is where all centralised efforts have failed.

Let us suppose for a moment that we could replace politicians with philosophers – ecologist philosophers. What means and criteria would this élite use to define all the needs and the means of satisfying them? Substituting 'eco-state' control for the dictatorship of capitalism and the market, or the dictatorship of the *nomenklatura*, would not make much difference.

The interests of capitalism and the state often combine, if only at the level of military-industrial complexes. *Nomenklatura* are the expression of an extreme form of state control.

Many of the problems faced by societies can only be solved if the following two conditions are fulfilled: firstly, the vast majority of people – in theory, all of them – must have a real possibility of defining their own needs and the responses to them, and of controlling the process from beginning to end; and secondly, that the solutions should be looked for at a local and regional level, firmly rooted in grass-roots experience which, thanks to the democratic and critical use of new information and communications technology, would be directly linked (with no short-circuits) to global facts.

A political reaction to ecological and social risks must, above all, be democratic, decentralised and participative, and as direct as possible. The greater the awareness of the interdependence of life and ecological and social problems, the greater the need for a right to diversity.

As we work out our needs and aims, the need to think globally, yet act autonomously will become increasingly acute.

The end of the nation-state

The nation-state must be replaced by smaller communities in a wider space. This is a daring suggestion. We do not have an array of ready-made solutions. In the abstract, one could conceive of Europe as one big whole which would include not only Spain, France, Yugoslavia, Poland etc., but also Catalonia, the Basque country, Corsica, Ireland, Kossovo, and all the 'small nations' which exist, with their own languages and cultures, inside or astride the boundaries of larger nations. In short, autonomous regions within a unified European continent.

It will be difficult to re-construct Europe in this way. National questions are always, at heart, culturally based.

In its widest sense, culture affects all individuals' personalities. In order to build our personalities, we need a subtle collection of relationships and reference points. All over the planet, under all kinds of régimes, nations are fighting for self-expression and rebelling against the utilitarian control and uniformity which has taken away their points of reference, their sociocultural fabric and their ecosystems. This groundswell may well grow further in the next century. It is a rebellion which will only bring freedom if it also demands the other elements of freedom.

Culture and territory do not necessarily cover the same areas. In Europe, there are many nationalities tangled up together. Europe must protect the right of all people to circulate freely and to make their home anywhere. How do we ensure this? We propose that on the one hand, forms of government must be as authentic as possible, able to evolve in the knowledge that close as they may come to reflecting cultural complexity, they can never encompass it in its entirety. On the other hand, all nationalities must be recognised; those which can do so will express themselves in political and territorial formulae, while others who may be too dispersed because of history or who are located within other cultural territories might organise themselves within more diverse and fluid politico-cultural communities, but without being discriminated against because of this. The essential elements are: language, education, freedom of thought and expression in words and images, and real freedom of religion and lifestyle – once more, tied to the other elements of freedom.

Neither feudal fragmentation, nor unification at the top only; a Europe made up of regions does not only mean not creating an authoritarian super-state, but also not replacing the current EC member states by a mosaic of smaller sovereign states. Under no condition may the totally free expression and self-determination of all the federated communities, and the people who make them up, be destroyed.

Will this be the end of politics? It could be, if politics were reduced to administrative matters. But conflicting aims and the existence of contradictions will probably feed the continuation of politics beyond the withering away of the state.

This kind of politics cannot be produced in its entirety by spontaneous activity and direct dialogue. Institutions will be needed. The problem lies in preventing these institutions from being or becoming autonomous seats of power within society. It is the separate, dominating states which must wither away, not politics.

What is required is not destruction, but construction; not to conquer the state, but to create and experiment continually with radically new political institutions. Never before has a solution of this type been put in place on such a large scale. Systems of power must disappear, the conscious and unconscious roots of domination must wither away, to make way for self-determination.

This is a historic task which will take a whole epoch; and the final shape of the outcome cannot be visualised in advance. If we are to advance down the path towards this breakthrough, our ideas must become a guide for our everyday actions.

5

A new view of social emancipation

In 1830, the European proletariat was oppressed, barefoot, did not have enough to eat, and had a life expectancy of only 30 years. From this proletariat came the Luddite movement, the uprising of the Lyon silk workers, the Silesian weavers, and the Paris Commune. Following the example of the workers in the United States, workers demonstrated every 1st May for an eight-hour working day. They lost the 1905 revolution in Russia, and for a while won something in that of 1917. They led the spartacist rising in Germany, the workers' councils in Hungary, the insurrections and the Long March in China, they fought in the Spanish Civil war and with Tito's partisans. On numerous occasions, these millions of women and men have seemed to be opening up a future of social freedom. The socialist, communist and extreme left parties have mobilised peoples, appropriated the leaders and the creative spirits, and have had considerable powers and means at their disposal. What have they done with them? Disillusionment is now as great as hope once was.

What we understand by socialism is not the particular expressions given to it by the parties claiming its name, but the vast historical movement which appeared around 1830, and crystallised around diverse currents before its major incarnation in the work of Marx and its extensions, and the numerous Internationals. These expressions have been a historical failure.

Classical social democracy voted for war credits in 1914. In the name of efficiency, the communist parties perpetuated the deepest flaws in the old social order – economism, state control, and the cynical, patriarchal techniques of power. The extreme left became marginalised, cut off from the living movement of the society. Planet-wide, the real movement has no more need for those kinds of socialism. They have had their day. But the current that they sparked off has not been extinguished. A part of the movement keeps it alive, at the same time demanding that it breaks the chains of productivism, patriarchy, and state, and goes beyond its own limitations to take part in a new wave of freedom.

Political ecology puts its finger on the essential causes of the failure of the various elements of the established left. The way in which human society interacts with ecosystems highlights the problem of social relationships. Anti-ecological economies have developed in certain types of societies. Radical ecological policies cannot be successful without being linked to radical social measures. Far from being an alternative to social emancipation, ecological politics requires, and needs to promote, its own emancipatory alternative. It urges us to look at the socialist movement in a wider, more open and thus more realistic fashion. For many women and men, including the signatories of this manifesto, it is difficult to go beyond ways of thinking and acting which have been their points of reference for many years. If we do not have the courage to do this, the hopes and struggles of millions of human beings, in whose steps we would like to follow, will have been for nothing.

The Euro-left?

There is no unified social-democratic aim. The social-democratic, socialist and labour parties have evolved in diverse political cultures and play different roles in different European countries. As the 1970s became the 1980s, the 'historical compromise' was broken in Italy, Thatcherism carried the day in Britain, and the German and Swedish social democrats went into eclipse. At the same time, socialist parties came into power in France, Spain, Greece, and, in a limited fashion, in Portugal. Ten years later, neo-liberalism seems to have passed its peak. But in no European country is there anything like a 'popular front' or a union of leftist parties. Important as it is, the green dynamic is still in a minority. Social democracy is trying to respond to the latest problems by restructuring itself. Several parties have suggested that this could form the basis for a new 'Euro-left'.

By the middle of the twentieth century, workers from several European countries had secured rights and privileges to which social-democratic ideas and policies contributed. The attempt at a restructuring and renewal of social democracy takes account of new concerns and changes inside society. Its constituent tendencies reflect, to a certain extent, the contradictions of such vast electorates. Is this enough for social democracy to arrive at fundamental solutions by itself? Such solutions imply a change in social relationships. Social democracy limits itself to trying to change capitalist societies at the margins. It accepts the capitalist framework unconditionally. It has simply put in a bid for perpetual capitalism. Even if it wanted to go further, it could not. It can only stay in business with the connivance of the forces of capitalism, some of whom seem to find this kind of compromise to their advantage, for instance over the last fifty years in Sweden, or since 1982 in France, or with Felipe Gonzales' socialists in Spain. As things stand, the unification of the EC hoped for by the majority of social democrats cannot succeed against the majority capitalist interests.

Many of the leading figures in the social-democratic movement have worked for a policy of non-alignment. The reformers of social democracy are aiming for international détente. But the majority of European social-democratic parties which are in power still follow policies in line with NATO, despite the recent dissolution of the Warsaw Pact. In Spain, the PSOE could have supported strong popular resistance to entry into NATO. But it ignored this opposition and joined. The French Socialist Party – like the Communist Party – has followed the national consensus on a military nuclear capability, and has encouraged the development of a neutron bomb, the 'Rafale' aeroplane project, arms sales, and the formation of Franco-German units. In Africa it pursues neo-colonialist policies. In Britain, the leadership of the Labour Party has dropped its commitment to unilateral nuclear disarmament.

The reformers of social democracy claim to be taking into account the dangers of quantitative growth that takes no thought for the effects on the ecosystem. Some social-democratic parties have accepted the abandonment of civil nuclear power, yet the French Socialist Party makes the whole population of Europe run the risks inherent in the first industrial-scale fast breeder reactor, and is building nuclear power stations at a manic rate. In Sweden, the abandonment of nuclear power is being questioned again.

The majority of social democrats advocate the 'Europeanisation of Europe'. But many of them tend to substitute Western European chauvinism for nation-state jingoism. For most of Europe, immigration policy consists of policing the frontiers. Some social democrats do not recognise the rights of Basques, Corsicans and other nationalities.

The majority of social-democratic parties criticised the neo-liberalism of Reagan and Thatcher. But their economic policies have swallowed a strong dose of neo-liberalism themselves. In Italy and Spain, they practise it in an almost pure form. They consider European integration to be above all the construction of a market whose sway they dream of extending to Central and Eastern Europe.

These parties generally criticise state control. But they often treat people like victims in need of assistance, or minors to be told what their needs are. Their interests identify more and more with those of the technocrats. In each country, they ally their own fate with that of the established political logic, which tends to suffocate any political renewal.

In France, a high level of state control is traditional, and the Socialist Party is keen to confine political activity to a simple left-right scenario. In Britain, the Labour Party participates in an antiquated system of parliamentary turn-taking, founded on an archaic electoral system, thanks to which a minority of under 40 per cent of votes can obtain a clear majority of seats in parliament. In Italy, the Socialist Party favours presidential rule. In Greece, PASOK has been sucked into corruption. To stick rigidly to structures means to reject any innovative projects outright. In Germany, the SPD rallied to the concept of German unification, which gave no thought to research into an ecological, democratic or social alternative.

After some thought, the Italian Communist Party – inasmuch as it still keeps the title – renounced Eurocommunism in favour of the 'Euro-left' ('sinistra europea'). The 'nuovo corso' (new path) adopted in 1989 supported the Gorbachev line in the eastern bloc countries, and considered the international communist movement to be outdated. It is developing its relations with the German SPD and other parties of the Socialist International, although it considers classical social-democracy to be a spent force. Its 'strong reformism' is very close to the new, improved social democracy. The Italian Communist Party is fighting to gain control of Italian reformist currents to create one large movement, rather than starting a second alignment within the Euro-left. It wants to bring about a great class compromise in Europe. It encourages new social movements, has taken a clear stance against nuclear power, and has stopped consigning women's issues to the fringe. It advocates détente, while still considering Europe to be the 'second pillar' of NATO. However, it is tending more and more to replace alternatives by a simple change at the top.

In short, the potential Euro-left seems to favour neo-Keynesian scenarios. It accepts capitalist structures, but tries to influence them with 'social guidance', also grafting an ecological accounting system on to growth. It aims for a single European market, for a redefinition of its relationship with the Third World that will create new markets, and for economic exchanges with the East.

Such scenarios are at least better than naked neo-liberalism, not to mention the barbarism of the extreme right. But we would be mistaken in thinking that the social-democratic, socialist and labour parties will be persuaded just by their own internal progressive tendencies to question capitalist, productivist, patriarchal, neo-colonial and statist principles. They can only be pushed towards this by a radical political dynamism outside their own ranks and outside the system, linked to the movements of all shapes and sizes which are questioning the very roots of the old society.

Our eco-socialist choice is not for the Euro-left, even if we do agree at times to co-operate with established left-wing parties on some matters to form new social and political majorities. Our first choice is to form an alliance of totally independent political forces to create our alternative.

The existing communist movement?

In none of the main capitalist countries have communist parties succeeded in changing society. They no longer have any chance of doing so. The wrestling-match which started in 1917 between the communist parties and the social-democrats has been lost by the communists. The political, economic, and ecological condition of the Soviet Union, Central and Eastern Europe, China and Vietnam shows that the crisis in all the countries governed by communist parties reaches into all domains. The Yugoslavian experiments into self-management have by and large been a failure.

The communists could have found methods and concepts in the works of Marx himself which should have allowed them to grasp ecological questions bodily rather than elude them, e.g. the dialectic method, the questioning of whether the right to property entails a right to exploit it in an unlimited fashion, and the concept of rational planning and control. Marx defines communism as a society where producers join together to regulate for themselves their exchanges with nature, in a rational manner. He insists on the necessity of shortening the working week, along the lines of the formula 'to each according to their needs'. He distinguishes quality from quantity, and use values from exchange values. Although he was ultimately contradicted by Stalin, he foresaw the withering away of the state. For him (and here again he was contradicted by Stalin), the free development of the individual is a pre-condition for the free development of society. Neither Marx nor Engels was ignorant of ecological questions. Quite an anthology of quotations can be gleaned from their work in which the economy appears as a flow of exchanges with the ecosystem. However, very early on, Marxist thought limited itself to looking at economic sub-systems in isolation. Only the internal contradictions of capitalism were looked at, without producing an alternative economic policy.

Post-Marxist thought has concentrated on two of the founder's theses: firstly, that social revolution necessarily erupts when, at a certain stage in their development, the material forces of production in society come into conflict with existing production relationships; and secondly, that communism cannot be attained after the revolution unless the forces of production have grown to such an extent that wealth is abundant. In other words, to change society, production must be increased as much as possible. This view has perverted the social imagination of a large part of the working population and its organisations. It has allowed anything which increases production or makes it more efficient to be called revolutionary.

Marx's criticism demystifies the relationships of production, not the forces of production. It is the latter which replace Hegel's *anima* as the driving force behind history – to such an extent that Lenin considered it obvious, beneficial, and unproblematic to import the forces of production created by capitalism lock, stock and barrel. With Stalin, the horrors of accumulation, which lasted five hundred years in the capitalist countries, were concentrated into a tenth of the time. The pace of social development was not determined by politics but by economics: a brutal forced march of five-year plans. Human beings were treated as a resource. Peasant cultures were wiped out. Whole peoples were forcibly removed. Camps where twenty million people died became an economic necessity: slaves to economic growth. A disproportionate importance was attached to heavy industry, to coal, steel and to dams. The aim was to change the geography of a whole continent in just a few years. On the threshold of the twenty-first century, many Marxists continue to believe that more necessarily leads to better. From the political anti-economy that it could have been, communism has turned into indiscriminate economism. Communism as it exists today is only the pursuit of productivity under another name. It is floundering under a mistaken development model, wasteful of energy and raw materials, and harmful to society.

At the same time, communism has shown itself to be a power-seeking philosophy. In 1939 Stalin invented the theory of the state for its own sake, and unleashed terrible repression. Communist parties have reproduced the hierarchical nature of society in politics, seeing themselves as 'avant-garde' repositories of the monopoly of leadership. They wanted to be instrumental in the creation of society and culture. They wanted to mobilise people and groups like armies. For a long time they considered themselves as sections of the International based in Moscow, and the majority of them used the existing nation-states as a framework for putting their strategy for state control into practice. These parties pushed the concepts of 100 per cent unity, discipline and activism to an extreme. Stalinists, Maoists, 'Pol-pot-ists', Castro-ists, have all attempted to eliminate all political opposition to their power – and, above all, communist opponents. The dictatorship of the proletariat has become the dictatorship of the secretariat. Theory has been reduced to second place after policy, only called upon to legitimise decisions after they have been acted on.

According to Marx, the growth of the forces of production does not constitute the only 'material element' of social upheaval. The 'formation of a revolutionary mass' is also needed. In his view, this emancipatory role falls to the working class.

The definition of this class is linked to relations of production, i.e. to the relations of women and men inside the material production processes in which they live. These relations are both necessary and independent of human will, and correspond to a degree of development determined by the forces of production. This is essentially an economist viewpoint.

The working-class movement of the nineteenth century was built on this unique contradiction: the opposition between capital and work. The harsh reality of the class struggle led Marxist theoreticians to consider violence as the inevitable 'midwife' of socialism. Lenin defined our century as the era of wars and revolutions. 'It is easy to confuse questions of revolutionary ethics with questions of strategy and tactics', declared Trotsky. Communists have displayed complete confidence in history. A number of them are now asking how they can re-align Marxism to incorporate the new phenomena of ecology and feminism from a class standpoint.

But can a theory which has been so thoroughly questioned by the very movement it is meant to interpret and represent be kept in its exclusive position? Is the general crisis in communism a coincidence, or does it have its roots in the theory itself? Is Marxism the only theory for which a practical demonstration is not required? Experience proves that a theory which, despite the efforts of Lenin to analyse imperialism, despite the movement of the 'peoples of the East', despite Mao Tse-tung, is still marked excessively by its European origins cannot solve all the problems of the planet. Europe was the cradle of Marxism because it was the birthplace of capitalism. Generations of communists have learnt the 'three sources' of the theory: British political economics, German philosophy and French revolutionary politics. Marx's thought ignored, and even despised, the cultures of Islam, China, and India. Socialist thought must recognise that what has developed – or will develop – in Europe cannot necessarily be transplanted to the rest of the world.

Experience shows that as our thoughts reflect our beings, the workers' culture of productivism results from the dialectical tug-of-war which simultaneously opposes and unites capitalism with the proletariat. Both come from the same mould: economism. Ecology and feminism are intervening to break the spell which binds the two. They are splitting up the pair, and thus allowing socialism to become fully itself, free at last from capitalist monoculture, anti-systemic, without themselves becoming new global theories (a danger which, in our view, must be avoided).

Experience shows that techniques are not neutral, but linked to the end product. A socialist society cannot simply borrow its forces of production from capitalism. It must invent its own alternative techniques, a new economic rationale and a new way of organising work.

Experience shows that state control of the means of production and exchange does not change anything by itself. According to Marx, socialism must be 'an association of free human beings'; abolishing private ownership of the means of production without abolishing the treatment of the workforce as merchandise will not truly put an end to capitalism. The 'socialist' countries have kept both wage-slavery and capitalism's separation of the producers from the social means of production. If a socialist country does not abolish the relationship between wage-earner and employer, it should at least alter it, by making sure that social ownership becomes a legal option for its citizens as producers, consumers and users. Furthermore, this should mean a political appropriation, allowing people to adjust production and the service industries to their own needs, and to the need for balanced exchanges with ecosystems.

Experience proves that contradictions which have never been resolved in any country still exist between generalised state control and the aim of extinguishing the state. Many bureaucrats do not see the management of the economy as their own responsibility. Conformity, servility, and even corruption take hold. Differing sectors of the state apparatus dispute economic power amongst themselves, with the same harmful effects as competition for profit. Bureaucratic impenetrability is no easier to see through than that of market forces. Militarisation is ruthless. On a more basic level, bureaucracy tends to confront workers in an extension of the logic of the class struggle, by dragging them into productivism. A socialist society must aim for integrated citizenship.

Experience proves that simply criticising individualism is limiting. 'Barracks communism', and seeing the nation as a factory, can cause intolerable suffering and alienation. It deprives society of immense reserves of initiative and ability. A socialist society should not just call on class consciousness, and neither should it rely on other collective awarenesses such as race or gender consciousness. Its only chance is to promote as much as possible the two humanising principles of 'the personal is political' and solidarity. Happiness cannot be programmed-in; it can only come about as an accompaniment to the welfare and fulfilment of each individual in the community.

Experience proves that the working-class movement has transformed many societies, but has freed none. If socialism allied itself solely with the proletariat of the big factories, it would have a short life. Ecology itself shows that the working class cannot be the only exploited group subject to unavoidable historical change. We are all – workers, consumers and users – alienated in our relations with nature and the economy.

No single contradiction carries within itself the seeds of the worldwide overthrow of the system. The one fact which is new in our era is that all the main contradictions are emerging simultaneously. Certain people and groups experience one contradiction more keenly than another, and become radicalised due to exploitation at work, or feminism, or ecology. Some contradictions are in opposition to each other. They are potentially so complex that they make a nonsense of any attempt to explain the world according to one theory, and call for action from a wide variety of social movements. A workerist viewpoint cannot be maintained in isolation, nor can one contradiction be replaced by another. The eco-socialist transformation that we are proposing will have many dimensions. It must allow us to move from a limited emancipation, which has failed, to freedom for everybody – a graveyard for the dogmas of the workers' movement, and a formidable challenge, both political and theoretical.

PART
TWO

What can we do?

First of all, how can we imagine the changes needed?

For two million years, a sort of implicit 'ecological contract' linked humanity with nature. The neolithic revolution changed the terms of this contract. Capitalism has torn it up brutally. Capitalism's tendency towards infinite growth continually stimulates production of goods and services, thus reducing their real value. It falsifies the rate of depletion of resources, and the rate at which waste is being produced. Society, the species, indeed all living things, are forced to bear the rising costs of unbridled growth. Capitalism's economic pattern, which it has spread throughout the world, is founded on the exploitation of the 'periphery' by the 'centre' – all over the world, nature and human beings are being exploited by a small, wealthy minority. The gap between capitalism and (insofar as it still exists in practice) socialism has an economic cause. Nowadays, it is often said that these two power-systems are growing closer – though their real similarity lies in their roots. They are twins, and their common traits are their exploitative relationship with nature, and their patriarchal base.

Their policies are the worst imaginable, and they will cost us dearly. A final catastrophe, ecocide and genocide together, is not unthinkable. In any case, serious damage is unavoidable. Tomorrow and beyond, the legacy of these policies will be severe. Thousands of years after the leaders of capitalism and communism are forgotten, ecologists unknown to us will still be trying to put right the problems that they will have inherited – for example, nuclear waste. Would a return to the old ways help? Throughout history, any return to old ways of doing things has been a complete disaster. The small number of people in Europe who survived the collapse of the Roman Empire needed six or seven centuries to emerge from the savagery that followed. Without the reconquest of Spain and the destruction of Andalusian civilisation, Islam and the West could have developed together. French society is still marked by the centralising, impoverishing, and levelling effects of the revocation of the Edict of Nantes. Deliberate regressions to inhumanity, in particular anti-semitism, have terrorised the twentieth century.

Ecological ideas stress the concepts of thresholds and

irreversibility. Since the 1950s, numerous thresholds have been overstepped, with irreversible effects. It would be senseless to try to restore the ways of life led by far less complex societies with far lower numbers of people, when ecosystems were far less disturbed. To break with our current way of doing things means, for us, drawing up a new 'ecological contract', which would open up a richer, more aware balance, but which would also, unlike a fully-planned techno-natural utopia, be more uncertain. It has been done in the past: agricultural techniques in Central Europe have re-created mixed forests after the originals had been razed; we are now trying to save the prairie created in America by the Indians after they had destroyed the virgin forest; we protect artificial lakes and woods; we rely on species such as maize, tomatoes, potatoes, soya and many others, which have travelled the world with humans in camel or wagon trains, or in ships.

The history of nature is not just natural, but social as well. Social relationships are also present. A new 'ecological contract' cannot avoid being a 'social contract' too. But should we wipe the slate, and start again from scratch? It is never possible to wipe the slate completely clean. Productivism cannot be halted, and even less reversed, by slogan or by decree. Existing fixed assets must be revitalised on a grand scale with new modes of production, new techniques, new materials, new settlements. Though the machines run at full speed, or, as is so often the case nowadays, at a surplus, the Earth's fixed assets are endowed with inertia. To what extent can we reverse techniques, agricultural and horticultural methods, our exchange mechanisms, and the structures which organise our lives such as housing and transport? Fixed assets have a considerable accumulated value, and not simply in market terms; what can be done to stop the 'dead wood' paralysing the living trees? How can their value be set to work in fundamentally new production and consumption processes? Current attempts at reconversion, admittedly only partial and hemmed-in by the system, have already shown on a small scale the difficulties of trying to revolutionise all levels of the economy within such constraints. For example, population growth makes ecological projects which involve only a small number of people illusory and/or immoral. The notion of limited resources, which like that of constraints is fully logical, was forgotten by the mathematicians of the Club of Rome. Throughout history, resources have evolved in line with scientific knowledge, technical innovation and lifestyles; thus, the percentage of plants and animals which have been domesticated, used, or even studied, is statistically tiny. But limits do exist, which will, for example, make it very difficult to increase resources enough simply to keep up with the primary needs of ten thousand million human beings. At the current level of expertise, we should not harbour too many illusions as to the possibilities of, for instance, harvesting food from the oceans.

Capitalism and communism as they exist today are not just ideas to be argued about. Multinationals, banks, economic polarisation, military-industrial complexes, all-powerful state apparatus, and *nomenklatura* are realities which are both massive and diversified, and which above all represent the interests of the powerful classes. If ecology ignored these realities, it would not be in a position to change anything. It cannot solve by itself all the problems which it uncovers. What are the forces which can be mobilised, now and in the future, to create an ecological socialism? It is society which decides in the last instance, not the forces of production, and not powerful minorities. Inertia is also deeply rooted in society: in the level and content of education and information available, and even more in the force of habit, in our lifestyles, and in our mentalities. The behaviour which leads to the most serious inertia is not an unbridled lust for consumption – and certainly not among the billions of poor people who ask only to live – nor the desire to dominate, but our acceptance of the thousand-year-old seizure of the right to decide by one sex, one class, one bureaucracy, one clan. The future will depend on whether or not billions of women and men are able to overturn these age-old structures and take control of their own lives. The speed, the extent, the limits and the contradictions of the changes in political culture which can be seen practically everywhere at present are the big unknown factors. No one knows if this march towards self-determination will proceed quickly, very quickly, or much more slowly. Human minds cannot be re-written like blank sheets of paper – no one has the skill or the right to do that. As a Chinese proverb says, 'passing feet will make the path'. It would be a miracle if current modes of production were to be overturned instantaneously all over the world. Experience shows that it is costly and useless to try and bring about this kind of miracle. Brutal transplants are not successful.

As eco-socialists, we reject the idea that catastrophes, whether spontaneous or provoked, can bring about desirable change. We consider that the break with presents ways can only be a complex and lengthy transition from one mode of production and life to others. These changes are, largely unforeseeable. They will probably not all take place at the same speed, but will include several stages of compromise of varying length between the various forces. Sometimes the pace will speed up, and sometimes it will seem as if it is in reverse. There will of course be contradictions, and possibly failures, but also continuations and innovations at the same time. At a given time, a number of different modes of production will exist side by side.

Why we choose nonviolence

'The atomic bomb,' said Albert Einstein, 'changed everything, except mentalities.' Violence is everywhere in today's world. The state has increased its power in society by exerting violence, and in order to exert it further.

The Pentagon, the Soviet and Chinese general staffs, and the British and French ministers of defence influence all kinds of decisions, for example the choice of energy sources. The military control large sectors of industry; they trade, maintain relations with their counterparts in other countries, and alter the course of scientific research. They consume vast quantities of raw materials, energy, food, land, and money. They monopolise human resources. They block democratic change. Armies fear that decentralisation will cause their version of defence to crumble. At the head of each of the nuclear states, a few individuals hold the power of life and death over the human race and all higher life-forms.

Until the middle of the twentieth century, a military victory permitted the achievement of political or economic aims which had been fixed before the battle. This scenario no longer has any meaning.

One per cent of the world's nuclear capacity would be almost enough, according to some calculations, to unleash a nuclear winter. Both Britain and France possess this terrible capacity. Pushed along by its own momentum, the arms race keeps passing threshold after threshold. Now it has reached space! Strategies become more and more irrational. The more complex a system becomes, the less controllable it is. Reaction times become shorter and shorter. The distinction between nuclear and conventional arms is becoming blurred. Military command centres (command, control, communications) are more and more vulnerable. Even if it were only limited to one region of the Earth, a nuclear war would not leave any 'sanctuary' unharmed. Repression and torture are becoming more widespread. Everywhere, the 'long arm of the law' (the police) is ready to grab. Propaganda renders people senseless, censorship mutilates and inquisitions massacre.

As eco-socialists, we choose to follow the course of non-violence. Nonviolence cannot change all political decisions. It cannot be applied in the same way in all situations. Sometimes, a people has no option but recourse to arms to save itself, for instance against fascism; but it should know then that it will have to pay the price. Nevertheless, there is a growing need for, and possibility of attaining, nonviolent societies. The great social changes we are hoping for involve studying and trying out all the possibilities of nonviolent action, in all situations. Nonviolence is a realistic policy. It opposes both civil and outside wars, and does not leave its citizens helpless in the face of others' hostilities.

Present-day states do not base their legitimacy just on democratic principles (such as human rights, and the sovereignty of the people). They are also founded on the archaic sanctification of violence, the glorification of armies and their chiefs, primitive myths about territory and/or race, the covert or open use of brutal force (the power of wealth, the apparatus of repression, administration and ideology). But modern states are finding it more and more difficult to get by without democratic legitimacy, in both internal and external politics. Western states are at pains to make sure that conflicts do not turn into major challenges to their legitimacy. Eastern European states have discovered this necessity too. The more the ideas of liberty, rights, openness, and control take a hold of people, the more they become real forces to be reckoned with. A policy of nonviolence relies on a strong consensus of protest, justice and sense of fair play to form a social movement which is stronger than the state. Nonviolence extends strike tactics to all social spheres by the use of passive resistance, non-cooperation, and boycotts. By using such policies, people learn. By putting into practice rights which the state does not recognise, or at most recognises without letting them be put into practice, civil disobedience uncovers the real illegitimacy of state oppression.

War and civil war are not the right anvil on which to forge a new kind of human being. The 'heroes' they produce are not the ideal builders of a free society. The strength of nonviolent action is in its constructive, non-combative nature. It requires higher levels of awareness, agreement, self-discipline and courage. This can be seen, for instance, in the Polish Solidarity movement, and in the Palestinian *intifada*. It brings into play independent groups, focused on tangible, agreed achievements. It brings together a wide variety of people, and allows a large number to take part in the action, even if they cannot take up arms. In short, it socialises politics more. Society thus learns to do without the state as much as possible, to deal with conflict by alternative methods and to envisage the end of all authoritarianism. It would be absurd to put off the implementation of such changes until after the revolution. Radicalisation can only be a long-drawn-out process, practical and open. On an international level, conflicts can no longer be solved by military force. The time has come to start an open, public debate throughout Europe (including the military) on collective security and alternative, nonviolent defence strategies. Real peace is better than just a lack of war. What we need is a new view of conflict and the way to solve it, fundamentally opposed to any form of social Darwinism.

Why we must act now

We do not want to close difficult theoretical discussions, for instance between ecology and social emancipation. But we believe that discussion should not delay our setting off down the road to the survival of the human species. To turn back because of the lack of a theoretical basis means compromising humanity's chances. What is more, we reject any attempt to formulate an official theory or a single philosophy. We must take a historical choice to take a different path. The practical task will be hard and long, and cannot wait for theory.

Our struggle for integrated citizenship

Integrated citizenship means, above all, *equal citizenship* without exceptions. Whoever lives in Europe should be considered as a citizen, with all the rights that go with citizenship, of which the most symbolic are the rights to vote, to choose candidates and to stand for election. This principle severs the link between citizenship and origin, class and sex. It is accepted in theory in Europe, but has still to be put into full effect. The innovation consists of separating citizenship from nationality, for immigrants as well as Europeans. Even if an age limit (perhaps 16) has to be set for the purposes of voting in political elections, it is still vital to consider all children as full citizens, possessing all fundamental rights from birth.

Integrated citizenship is, as far as possible, *direct citizenship*. The modern state depends on the delegation of power: citizens delegate their theoretical sovereignty to elected representatives, and these representatives delegate a part of this delegated power to the administrative apparatus. Any system which functions mostly in this way removes power from the majority of its people. The tendency of institutions to exist for their own sake, supported by technological structures and large electronic media, accentuates this confiscation. At the same time, societies are becoming more and more complex, and each decision can affect the present and future lives of millions, indeed billions, of people. Our eco-socialist project must take into account this contradiction between a representative state and direct democracy. To transcend it means both changing the existing state institutions and apparatus (including political parties), and at the same time increasing direct democracy at all levels, in ways as yet unimagined. Each situation will require all the issues to be set out and examined. We will have to fight all attempts to make politics into a profession.

Integrated citizenship means *solidarity*. Citizens are not isolated individuals. In most cases, self-determination has to mean co-determination. If we do not join together, the law of the jungle will ensue, bringing with it powerlessness and the return in force of authoritarianism. Co-operation, working out aims together and common control require us to relate to each other in many different kinds of groups and networks, some permanent, some temporary, many of which have still to be invented. The very concept of democracy calls on us to think.

History has shown over and over again that minorities, or even individuals, have often been right in their opposition to the vast majority, or represented a heritage worth preserving. It has shown that the agreement of the majority to big programmes has often been more formal than real. Democracy is therefore only conceivable if it looks for as wide and as real a consensus as possible, yet taking into account dissenting views and accepting different opinions and experiences, and leaving the maximum degree of liberty to groups and individuals within any areas of agreement.

Integrated citizenship means *all-embracing citizenship*. Instead of a division between civil equality, which is recognised, and socio-economic equality, which is not, citizenship can be shared but not divided. Self-determination should link and encompass all domains. There will no longer be any place of work which can write over its door: 'Here you cease to have rights'. Nowhere outside the workplace where you will find written up: 'Production methods are none of your business'. Civil rights must be extended to all spheres of society. Already some struggles and some aspects of the new social movements reflect a wish on the part of workers (both men and women) to take more control over their working lives. Unfortunately, some of these attempts have been led astray by management, in both private and public enterprise. But what we call 'self-management' in English and 'autogestion' in French cannot be confined to companies, any more than the German 'Selbstverwaltung' can be confined to communes. All society must be free to make its own pronouncements on its aspirations and needs, at the same time providing itself with the means to make its choices known and respected. This can only happen if we create a complex, evolving network of exchanges through which people can work out and express their own choices. For example, ideas can be researched and synthesised at community, regional and Europe-wide level, but also through associations, Friendly Societies, trade unions (new-style) etc. The state and businesses have taken on a life of their own; their functions must now be integrated into society. Society should itself regulate the economy and politics, subordinating them to control by the citizens.

This means that integrated citizenship must be *ecological*. It can only develop through a series of exchanges between society and the ecosystems, part of a conscious, increasingly rational attempt by citizens working together to solve the problems. These exchanges will strengthen ties, both within societies and between human societies and nature.

We say: *a creative citizenship is an evolving citizenship*. Integrated citizenship can never be limited to the current state of affairs. Its content, form and practice will transform citizenship itself (within the bounds of natural, biological and sociological laws). Integrated citizenship is an open-ended process. Self-determination, i.e. the free development of individuals, will be self-productive (to steal a phrase from cybernetics) of the free development of society.

Whether they crush or flatter them, states and politicians will always be against those who want to change politics in this fashion. Will society set aside selfishness, the desire to dominate, and aggressiveness so easily? Some analyses of the state reduce its dominance to the defence of certain class and bureaucratic interests. Western states are, in a sense, an administration for the general affairs of the bourgeoisie; eastern bloc states have been the tools of the *nomenklatura*. But state domination can also be explained by an acceptance, even a need, on the part of the dominated. Force and propaganda are not a sufficient basis; there must also be consent. Ecology too leads us not only to ask the question, 'Why do we produce so many harmful products?', but also, 'Why do people want them?' To reduce this acquiescence to clever deception using media publicity would be only to skim the surface of reality. The market society and the production models of East and West inculcate false values; but why do they manage to? Such questions are not asked in traditional politics, and with reason! If we are to change the basis of politics, it is essential that these questions are examined and debated from all angles and using all possible approaches. Integrated citizenship means that everyone is *responsible*. Some ecological, social and cultural movements have started to tackle these questions. At the moment, those in power are still able to answer them plausibly. But little by little, human values are subverting their activities.

Unprecedented global possibilities

The risks are high. But so are the possible rewards. Humanity still has some margin for manoeuvre. We can use the flaws in the system. Potent changes are taking place in societies, and the new social movements have a long history. New lifestyles are taking shape. How many will succeed? How many will fail? All societies can take advantage of the diversity of life to create whatever new approaches suit them – provided that their members learn to 'hear the grass grow'.

Productivism is in crisis – not only in financial and budgetary crisis due to over-production, and not only a crisis in government, ethics and drug abuse; capitalism has known many such. Neither is it only a crisis of poverty, planning and alcoholism; the Eastern European countries have been fighting these for a long time. The crisis is in the roots of the system which are common to both régimes. The fundamental weakness of productivism is that it treats the human workforce and nature purely as raw materials, without however being able to produce them for this purpose. (Though they dream of it: hence the dabbling in genetic manipulation.) This weakness affects accumulation.

By the end of the 1960s the crisis in Taylorism and Fordism was apparent in the capitalist countries. New demands were emerging in the fight for better working conditions. These went far beyond the classic problems of health and safety. The whole concept of work as exploitation was questioned, with its detrimental effects on individuals' lives, their health (in the wider sense as defined by the World Health Organisation), on the rhythms of their lives, on their potential. This new radicalism carried within it the seed of a vision which goes beyond the reductionist view of exploitation at work which has impregnated the workers' movement, which boils down to the levying of value-added deductions from the monetary value of the wealth created by workers. At almost the same time, the ecological movement began to question the levies made on nature, and feminism was challenging patriarchal values in the economy and in all areas of life. Patriarchy, the bureaucracy and technocracy first noticed the crisis in Taylorism, then the crisis in the relationship between productivity and nature and the crisis in the worldwide relationship between the centre and the periphery. They are now trying to reorganise work patterns.

Economists have already made attempts to work out new theoretical tools, for instance the concept of social cost, or the principle of 'economicity' of François Perroux and Henri Bartoli, in which the lesser ecological and human costs are taken into account when covering the majority of human costs.

In 1987 UNICEF proposed some changes in the indicators used to calculate gross national product. Reports by the Club of Rome and Dag Hammarskjöld in the 1970s, the North-South commission headed by Willy Brandt (1980), the CNUCED report, the Worldwatch Institute and the Brundt-land Report (1987) all bear witness to a growing awareness. Even the World Bank has had to recognise that the solutions it has so far advocated have not managed to defuse bombs such as the debt crisis.

The system is growing so huge that it is finding it difficult to keep control, despite new developments in control mechanisms. If things carry on as they are, in one or two generations, there will be 6, 8, or 10 billion people, all different; 3, 4 or 5 billion young people under the age of 20; 8 to 10 times (or more) the military capacity to wipe out all higher life-forms on the planet; mechanised factories equivalent to 40, 50 or 60 billion slaves; huge cities; and a hundred billion dollars or more speculated each day by world business on stock exchanges and currency exchanges. The decision-makers still think in the archaic terms of power and profit, and universalised solutions. These wooden ideas must be dismantled by taking all possibilities into account, by thinking in terms of open-ended processes and a wide range of choices, by rethinking needs and inventing radical innovations, and at the same time paying a proper respect to the intelligence and initiative of billions of human beings.

Although capitalism is built on the ruins of other modes of production and ways of life, the world economy has not become totally homogenous. There is still a tangle of relationships and interchanges between systems. Other forms of production shatter the weak links in the chain: the domestic economy, i.e. two billion women already; part of the agricultural economy, i.e. over a billion peasants (mostly women); regional or local economies within which nationalist sentiments and independence movements flourish; new types of economies such as the co-operative sector or truly alternative experiments (rare, even in Asia, Africa and Latin America and Oceania where they are growing in number and significance).

Forces of production and lifestyles are moving closer together. But this does not mean that societies are becoming more homogenised; on the contrary, their complexity is increasing. Diagrams which try to summarise society in two or three major classes and a few intermediate layers or categories are further and further from reality. The plurality of elements and relationships in society is ever-growing, while information, people and goods are circulating more and more intensively. This is fertile ground for the growth of creative interactions between an endless variety of social forces.

On a planetary scale, the number of paid workers in manufacturing and service industries is growing. In Poland, Hungary, East Germany and Czechoslovakia, they demonstrated their ability to take new political and trade union action. Part of their motive force has given a boost to the social movements in the West. The peasantry has an enormous part to play in a physiologically vital question – agriculture. Feminism has barely started its work. As questions of culture, education and information become central, intellectuals and students take key roles in the radical movements. Their role was decisive in the collapse of the dictatorship of Central Europe.

For the first time in many years, momentous changes are rocking Central and Eastern Europe and the Soviet Union. Should we help these countries to pass from state productivism to capitalist productivism in one shape or another? In our opinion, this mode of production has confronted the peoples of Eastern Europe with the same problems as the rest of Europe is facing. We propose a completely different type of mutual aid and coming together: the reorientation of our respective societies towards ecological and humane ways of production and life. This could include the utilisation of economic instruments such as the market, or planning – but always in a subordinate position.

For better or for worse, our futures are interdependent. The peoples of Eastern Europe have everything to gain from the development of an eco-socialist dynamic in Europe. Failure to do so in the East, in favour of some bureaucratic or capitalist form of productivism, would handicap eco-socialist transformation in the West. Eco-socialism needs *perestroika* and the other changes which have started in Eastern Europe to succeed, and to turn towards self-managed, pacifist and ecological forms of socialism.

Many westerners were unwise enough to declare that Soviet society could not be changed, and that indeed it had vanished under the weight of the all-powerful state. This society has now started to demonstrate that it is far from dead. Nationalist demands are being expressed after decades of suppression and assimilation. The desire for liberty and openness contrasts starkly with the bureaucracy of the state. Both Stalin and Brezhnev ware unable to suppress environmental concerns. In 1926, the scientist V. I. Vernadski synthesised a whole current of scientific research with his theory of the biosphere. Societies for the protection of nature were founded in 1924, and by 1984 had 34 million members. The battle of Lake Baikal began over 20 years ago. Hydro-electric projects and other industrial projects in the Volga basin attracted opposition. Moscow citizens signed petitions in the 1960s for factories which produced pollution to be re-sited. In 1981, the *samizdat* circulated a pamphlet by Boris Komarov entitled *The Red and the Green*, an indictment of the destruction of nature in the Soviet Union. Since then groups (such as 'Green World' led by the chief editor of *Novy Mir*, Sergei Zalygin), publications, and local committees have grown and multiplied.

It is possible that ecological, energy and economic problems may put a physical limit on the extent of the reconstruction that Mikhail Gorbachev is attempting. But in the first instance at least, the economic difficulties which restructuring has brought with it have not caused great popular uprisings such as the conservative apparatchiks and western economists had predicted. Human beings have proved themselves superior to such a contemptuous opinion of them; human beings do not live by bread alone. Even in poverty, Soviet citizens, Poles, Hungarians, Czechs and Romanians, like the Chinese, fought in the first instance for independence, their own culture, liberty and justice. It is now possible to imagine socialism without steel, and even more without nuclear weapons; but without democracy and human values there will never be true socialism.

Even before *perestroika*, the main dissident groups in the Soviet Union and Eastern Europe, and some of the alternative movements in the West, had become aware that they were fighting the same battle. After the great waves of support for *Solidarnosc* throughout Europe, the Euromissile crisis and the rebirth of the peace movement put the dissidents, and even the officials, of the East in contact with western pacifists. On the one side, they became aware that they were part of a Europe-wide movement; and on the other side, it was realised that the stalemate which had resulted from the second world war could be unfrozen. They began to find themselves reunited not only on the objective of human rights, but also on peace and then the environment.

In the mid-1980s, the Strategic Defence Initiative ('Star Wars') programme initiated by President Reagan came up against the resistance of a large part of the scientific community and public opinion. In the 100 American universities most active in research, over half of all the physicists put in writing their refusal to sign contracts linked to this project. In Western Europe, the peace movement developed outside the sphere of control of the international communist movement. It began to question all power-based politics, and to favour worldwide nonviolent organisation. Pacifists from Eastern Europe, newly freed from the control of communist apparatus, also came into contact with this concept for the first time. At the same time, the leaders of the two superpowers took stock of the risks and economic costs inherent in the arms race; the Reagan-Gorbachev agreement included, for the first time, the destruction of existing weapons. Slowly and with difficulty, a new détente is beginning, regional conflicts are being settled and the legacies of the second world war and the cold war are beginning to be cured.

On 7 December 1988, Mikhail Gorbachev made a speech to the United Nations General Assembly: firstly, on the need to invent 'a fundamentally new basis for the functioning of the world economy', with 'a new structure to the international division of labour'; and secondly, on the growing threat of environmental catastrophe. 'The world economic crisis has uncovered the contradictions in and the limits of the traditional style of industrialisation'. Are these views compatible with the promotion of nuclear power and grandiose projects such as that to increase electricity production in Siberia and the eastern extremities of the Soviet Union by a factor of 2.6, oil extraction by 3.1 to 3.8 times, and gas by a factor of between 7.2 and 9.3? The debate has begun. It is most important that it be held simultaneously in Moscow, Prague, Warsaw, Budapest, Sofia, Berlin, Paris, Madrid, London, Rome, Stockholm, Dublin, Ajaccio and many more. It is essential that it should not be limited to political circles, but should encompass all parts of society.

Under these conditions, now that the situation is much more open, we propose to build an alternative strategy for the part of Europe in which we live. This strategy, and what it will achieve, will be the opposite of a market dominated by capitalist accumulation, and will continuously strive to communicate with, listen to and co-operate with all the other peoples of

Europe, and, if possible, widen this manifesto to include projects able to tackle their specific problems. The four main directions that this strategy will take are: resistance, reflection, reorientation, and joint action.

Resistance

The most urgent priority is to preserve whatever can be preserved, to intervene as early as possible before irreversible damage turns to tragedy. The longer we wait, the more difficult it will be.

This pre-supposes that we have or can develop systems for constantly observing the ecosystems and the way they inter-relate, to find out the maximum of information on all the variables. Such observations would have to be made in large numbers, the findings would have to be publicised, and the connections would have to be demonstrated and interpreted. Such exacting but essential work must not be left to the official economic and state experts alone. All the fine sifting will only have a point if this interdisciplinary research into all the effects of human activity is undertaken both in the scientific com-munity and in the population at large, in collaboration with associations, trade unions, local councils, and various professions.

Such a technique can be used at all levels, on a wide variety of subjects: a factory, a dam, a motorway, an industrial process, a product, a district of a town, a tree . . . Restrictions, moratoriums, or bans can be obtained; civil disobedience, boycotts, blockades can be used. In the global vision which we are encouraging, to defend the very day is to be a visionary; to safeguard your immediate locality is to protect the whole Earth.

The present movement has highlighted a few widespread stumbling blocks.

Racism

Immigrants play a full part in European societies, and call the attitudes of these societies into question. In many countries, immigrants have formed their own associations and are part of the social movements. They are helping society to move.

As eco-socialists, we do not see why Europe should be primarily white. The double paranoia of falling birth rates and the closure of frontiers has its roots in racism, and in the desire to carry on exploiting the Third World. In Europe we have ample space, resources, and a climate which up to now has been mild. There are not enough young people.

Immigrants must be able to pass freely from one country to another, and to be able to choose how and where they wish to live. At present, they are more or less completely denied citizenship. They must be able to participate as equals, both men and women, in decisions. Cultures can evolve, mix and enrich each other. Exclusion, confrontation and assimilation waste this creative potential. All cultures must have the means to express themselves fully. European peoples have no scores to settle with Islam.

The rise of the extreme right in several European countries expresses an attempt on the part of the system to resolve its crisis at the expense of people of low social standing and from the Third world, by reactivating the racist, chauvinist and sexist ideas and sentiments which lie dormant in society, particularly in certain social strata. The economic and political opportunism of the established left has not provided a credible alternative. The French Communist Party, for example, flirted with anti-immigration policies for a few years; the German Social Democrats pussyfoot around the right to vote; the French Socialist Party still refuses to grant it. The point is not to gain ideological Brownie points, but to solve concrete problems. We are ready to look at the whole question of immigration, and to discuss it with anyone, especially immigrants.

The current tendency of Japan and the United States to move the 'world axis' towards the Pacific risks marginalising Africa. Europe must take on the responsibility for reversing this trend. European multinationals must also be persuaded to stop participating in the genocide of the Amazonian Indians.

Anti-semitism is one specific kind of barbarity. In several European countries – in the West, but also in Poland and in Russia – it is re-appearing in guises which must be fought with determination. Any weakness or ambiguity in this respect is criminal.

The arms race

Europe is the most nuclearised and militarised region in the world. This is where NATO and the former Warsaw Pact met. However, these two blocs have managed to export their armed conflicts to the Third World. We must seize the opportunity offered by the changes in the Soviet Union and central Europe to continue, speed up and widen the disarmament process which is still in its infancy, without becoming embroiled in the fragile, dubious concept of 'balance', and without refusing to take controlled unilateral measures. We reject any new weapons of war in Europe. All nuclear weapons must be destroyed. All chemical and biological weapons must disappear. Great Britain and France must give up their 'deterrents' immediately. The Soviet Union must reduce its conventional forces drastically. We must go beyond 'bloc logic'. All foreign forces must leave Germany. The Soviet and American armies must withdraw behind their frontiers. The states of Western Europe must actively contribute to the dismantling of NATO. The united Germany is over-armed: there must be a massive reduction in the number of troops – including police – and in all kinds of weapons.

Conflicts in Africa, the Middle East, Asia and Latin America where the superpowers and European states are implicated must be resolved as quickly as possible. We are opposed to arms sales in principle. Those countries which still have colonies must recognise their independence, and the army of occupation must withdraw from Northern Ireland. The transformation of international relations will be a long haul, and will demand a strong, independent peace movement.

Nuclear power

Our condemnation of nuclear energy is not on purely technical grounds. Rejecting nuclear power requires a society with more ingenuity, more decentralisation, and more subtlety. Already the people of Sweden, Italy and Austria have voted in referenda for the end of nuclear power. The Germans have succeeded in halting the construction of a nuclear reprocessing plant at Wackersdorf, but not their participation in the expansion of the one at The Hague. The fast breeder at Kalkar has not yet received its licence. The United States has abandoned the fast-breeder path. Europe must cease building nuclear power stations. Public opinion in the East must now join the debate.

Apart from a few low-powered prototypes, there are now two fast breeders in the Soviet Union, one in Japan, one at Dounreay in Scotland and two in France (*Phoenix* and *Superphoenix*). In November 1987, 200 delegates from ten countries formed the NENIG (Northern Europe Nuclear Information Group) to oppose the Dounreay fast breeder. They were supported by the government of the Faroe Islands, the local authorities of the Shetlands and the Orkneys, Iceland, Greenland, and 17 of the 19 regional councils in Norway. Campaigns against Dounreay Expansion (CADEs) were formed.

After just a few years on line, the amount of radioactivity put out by the Superphoenix adds up to several billion ALIs (Annual Limits of Intake, i.e., according to the official experts, the maximum dose of radioactivity that an individual can receive in one year without endangering his/her health, at least in the short term). If the Superphoenix continues functioning at this level, the total will exceed that of Chernobyl by a long way. A hundred years after the reactor is shut down, there will still be several tens of billions of ALIs. Damage resulting in the loss of coolant could cause the nuclear reactor to blow up. Such an accident could result in some of the radioactive contents being dispersed in the environment: the consequences for Switzerland, France and the rest of Europe would be appalling.

The use of fast breeder reactors on a large scale would require the separation, handling and transport of hundreds of tonnes of plutonium. Just as a microgramme of this product is deadly to human beings. A few kilos of plutonium are enough to manufacture a nuclear bomb.

We demand that the ten fast breeders already in existence on this planet be shut down immediately. The European Fast Breeder programme must be halted, and all the bodies set up to put the projects into effect must be disbanded.

Genetic manipulation

All modification of organic life can produce unforeseen and unwelcome effects. But research in this area is progressing fast, and the road from experimenting on mice to applications for humans is short. The risks involved in altering the human species seem much greater than any chances of improving it. Cloning and the introduction of genes to modify individuals to profit some government, production method or ideology are technically possible.

In our opinion, the necessary steps are:

1 To open a public debate, in which all arguments are clearly documented, as soon as any doubt exists on the use of any type of genetic research. Use of this research should be forbidden as long as the debate has not ascertained with sufficient certitude that the technique in question is harmless to humans and ecosystems;

2 To declare any attempt to alter the genetic heritage of the human race illegal, given the current level of knowledge.

On a related topic, we consider that no part, cell, tissue or organ from the human body should be used as a source of profit. To take or buy any of these parts from another person is a crime.

Animal rights

The richness of the bio-ecology is made up of the diversity of its species. Diversification is the law of ecology, which in this respect is directly opposed to the productivist law of standardisation. Gene banks are not enough to safeguard our genetic heritage. It is difficult to re-introduce species into modified environments. It is better to conserve these species in their proper habitat, to enrich them and to help them to evolve.

Animals are victims of productivism. We only have a poor idea of the suffering caused, at least above a certain level in the animal kingdom, by industrial livestock-rearing practices, slaughterhouses, and hunting, which present ecological problems due to the interdependence of all living things, and which are also contrary to the values of nonviolence. A legal statute must be introduced to protect animals from all forms of cruelty. Experimentation on animals must be strictly limited to cases where it can be demonstrated that no other means exists of resolving biological and/or medical problems.

General measures

We can begin to undermine the productivist model by taking some generalised steps, for example:

• Introducing the right to resist attacks on the ecosystems and on the integrity and potential of human beings into the Universal Declaration of Human Rights; such attacks are crimes;

• Fighting for a code of ethics on economic and technical decision-making; freedom of information; compulsory, open debate before any choice is made, with all sides having access to the same resources and the encouragement of the right to protest; the institution of bodies of expertise which are independent of economic and state power; opposition to advertising pressures which create new needs and desires, in particular by a requirement to publish critical results of tests and by developing counter-publicity; legal procedures and/or the right to appeal, both collective, such as a referendum from a popular initiative, and individual.

All these are not just abstract wishes. Here and there, things are beginning to happen, in response to demands expressed in societies.

In many cases, these blows for an end to the power of money, state domination, or technocratic arrogance will call for the sharing of information and long debates with scientists, technicians and workers. It is only if we are frank in sharing the problems with them that we will be able to research alternatives and join together to create a new concept of progress.

2

Reflection

We challenge the assumption that 'as soon as science is born, thought dies' (Heidegger). In our opinion, rationality is an indispensable adventure. The difference between humanity and the other species is that we can make use of our ability to think to bring about a fundamental and vital change in the way we act.

So often nowadays, science is allied to powerful political, economic and military interests largely concentrated in the wealthy countries. It is also still dominated by men. It produces knowledge, but increasingly lacks a coherent, global vision.

What emerges is not rationality. Productivism is an obsessive and narrow way of thinking, which conceals irrationality on a global scale. The positivist outlook which it engenders uses reason as a pretext for preventing the triumph of reason. Few people take the time to stop and think. We are impelled not by a passion for knowledge, nor even a taste for technology, but by speed and competition – even more formidable irrationalities.

Feminism and movements for social freedom and against political alienation ask fundamental questions of and about science.

Ecology is, we believe, the exact opposite of obscurantism. It shows us that we suffer from a lack of knowledge, not from a surfeit. With global ecology we are entering into new realms of research where the margins of uncertainty are growing wider. The size, the complexity and the interrelatedness of the phenomena at work in societies and ecosystems defy our straitjacketed ways of thinking. They make us recognise the relationships between the known and the unknown: each discovery raises new questions never thought of before. They demonstrate how different effects combine, interact and cascade together. Any variation in one ecosystem brings about changes in others. All things are shown to be both causes and effects. The effects are often only perceived too late. They sometimes appear to be positive – before we realise the harm they cause.

Global ecology, like many other branches of science nowadays, brings, or seeks, new concepts to understand complexity, finiteness, movement, emergence; the impossibility of reducing everything to its component parts; interaction, interdependence in time and space . . . It asks us to affirm new ways of thinking, such as the dialectic between quantity and quality, and to put our acquired notions and old ways of thinking into new contexts, such as Descartes' analytical ideals or Bacon's experimentation. With courage, anyone can renounce old thinking habits. But today we must all make much greater use of our liberty.

Humanity needs to think of radical new theories, independent of any control, censorship or conformity, in order to find ways of understanding which can adapt to the unprecedented problems that we have created.

No single new unitary theory has yet emerged. We are not even certain that such a theory is now possible, or desirable. The tendency to universalise solutions has dominated thought for a long time; we are certain that it misses a whole area of reality. Concrete examples of the singular, the diverse, and the unexpected spring to mind easily. Surely extreme complexity and movement have to be dealt with using different, sector-based theories, linked by common strands? Making the links would then become the crucial problem. New syntheses are needed in order to progress towards actual projects. They can only result from processes, to become processes themselves: devoid of all mystique, incomplete, open to questioning, leaving unknown and unexplained factors honestly as they are, using the gap between theory and reality to increase theoretical understanding by practical application.

Science cannot transcend societies. All science develops both according to intrinsic laws, and according to a mixture of social determinants and relationships: power, mentalities and mechanisms, as well as concrete economic and political choices.

All science depends on its method of pinpointing and asking questions; powerful decision-makers should not be the only ones to enter into dialogue with it! Science needs to come out of the laboratory; financiers, industrialists and bureaucrats should not be the only ones to bring it out! Some scientists are exploring ways of bypassing these channels. Informing, studying and working out solutions must become a collective task, albeit a huge one.

Scientific truth must be proven in practice; yet truth cannot be reduced to scientific and technical practice. Our theories must be proven in society as a whole.

The elaboration, theory and application of science can no longer remain the preserve of a tiny minority who possess the key to knowledge, unaccustomed to communicating and co-operating, even among themselves. The scientific community must be widened to include the whole of humanity.

This pre-supposes efforts to educate and inform, as well as to get rid of all secretiveness and élitism, whether acknowledged or not. All data banks must be open to all, and de-centralised, free to co-operate and display their differences.

It also pre-supposes that all areas of knowledge are examined with equal curiosity and openness. Knowledge which had been scorned for centuries and considered eccentricity has sometimes been the key to great discoveries (e.g. electricity or the genetics of maize); important and diverse knowledge and expertise have often been built up by ordinary people (e.g. peasants' agricultural practices; workers' production methods, including skilled workers and artisans; traditional medicines, etc.). Above all, science must undo all its links with authority. The only way for it to gain a higher cultural status and to help societies to enter a new era is to assert its critical function and to reject state control.

3

Reorientation

New structures are the core of any alternative project. To start turning things upside down, and progress from static to dynamic ecology, is the most important, but also the most difficult thing to do. Experience shows that structures can outgrow themselves. Within a few decades, changes can overcome inertia. Japan has changed virtually out of all recognition in less than a century. The United States took just a few years to become computerised; France took less than a generation to change its energy producing system; Italy and France took scarcely longer to become urbanised. Apart from these hackneyed economist models, it is possible to propose new ways of interacting, different ratios, other links between production and social usefulness.

We can start to change direction straight away by taking measures to reduce waste; slow down, save energy, stop using 'disposable' and short-lived products, bleached paper, tropical timber, fur, ivory, etc., etc. Industry could reduce the amount of water it uses in steel-making from 200 to 2 cubic metres per tonne; in paper-making from 1,000 to 80 cubic metres per tonne of pulp, and from 40 to 0.1 cubic metres per tonne of processed goods.

The signatories of this manifesto invite any person or group to take part in these thought processes, whatever their opinion of the manifesto as a whole and/or the rest of the proposals which follow. These first suggestions are far from being the outlines of a comprehensive programme. We are consciously limiting ourselves to a few aspects. We consider it no less important to foster thought and debate on such vital questions as education, culture and information. We would particularly welcome the views of young people on these topics.

Time and work

No alternative project can avoid the question of work. Any compromise on the management of the ecosystem which leaves those currently in charge of the economy in charge of finding a solution to the problem of paid work is irresponsible. The work ethic (where work means paid work for economic ends) is a fairly recent phenomenon in history. It infuses most men and many women with its ideology, and is inculcated by the majority of educational institutions. However, the concept is becoming obsolete in Europe. Nevertheless, paid work will continue to occupy a large part of adults' lives for a long time to come. The work question is, and will remain, central to their preoccupations.

In present society, unemployment destroys lives. Massive unemployment will not lead to an overturning of values for the better. A forced increase in leisure time, which excludes them from the activities which provide their social and financial standing, desocialises and destroys individuals. Here too, worse does not lead to better. We will not remove paid work from its central place in society by exacerbating the gap between rich and poor. As long as paid work is seen as a benefit which unemployed people are deprived of, it will be over-valued. The exclusion of unemployed people from society can only lead to a viable alternative if they are able to re-invest themselves in activities which they are in control of, and which are socially useful in a tangible way. Experience shows, however, that in the majority of capitalist countries where it has been tried, such a solution is a precarious one because it leads to low pay and reduces the bargaining power of those excluded from paid work. We can only humanise values by re-absorbing the unemployed.

All the western states have rejected full employment. It has never been reached spontaneously, but requires positive action from societies. In our view, full employment, like education, is the responsibility of society, not individuals. In order to attain it, social groups must alter their economic calculations and their scales of values. In Europe, full employment is impossible without a big reduction in the length of the working week.

The double crisis in Fordism and productivism is leading to agonising splits between employers, workers, consumers and end-users.

Workers have no chance of ending their exploitation if they concentrate their struggles on the part of their labour which comes back to them as wages. Ecology cannot even begin to transcend current production methods if it confines itself to the exterior of production and pays no attention to working conditions. The way in which we tackle work problems will affect the solutions to all the other problems. Full employment as we propose it must be on a humane, ecological basis.

Capitalism has proved in the last hundred years that it can absorb drastic reductions in the working week, by seeing it as a way to expand production, or as a mechanism for adjusting the monetary relationship between capital and labour. If the vicious capitalist circle is to be broken, a reduction in the working week must not be seen in economic terms. Even if it were not necessary to re-absorb unemployment, the working week would have to be considerably reduced anyway. Time is a vital human need, for women and men and for society. The level of productive forces in Europe makes possible a new kind of accumulation, based on an increase in free time. Once a sufficient income is assured to everybody, the best defence against pressures to consume ad infinitum is to aim for this kind of accumulation rather than a constant increase in the production of merchandise and in purchasing power to buy it.

The system of salaried work has separated time spent on industrial production and in the service sector from other forms of work necessary for the production and maintenance of human life: above all domestic work. What we refer to here as 'work sharing' is not the division of all paid work amongst the whole job market, but an equal sharing of all paid and domestic work between women and men. As for agricultural work, it too includes a large amount of work done by women which is not accounted for in monetary terms. The problem of how long is spent on agricultural work has to take into account some leeway for self-management, variations in labour-intensity between different methods used, and seasonal factors, and can only be resolved by developing combined measures such as increasing the number of farmers, putting a brake on competition to increase output, and a policy of continuous training and more leisure opportunities. Payment for farm work must be reconsidered, and integrated into the global picture of work carried out for the general good.

To limit the work question to time spent on it is to look at only one aspect. In the tradition of classical economics, in general work can be defined as the production of merchandise by merchandise. Work as expenditure of human activity is absent from the Keynesian macro-economic analysis, which is based on the quantity of work done. Such calculations reduce work to a time-package whose contents are not important. Marx distinguished between 'concrete' and 'abstract' work. In capitalism, the different types of merchandise – human and mass-produced – are exchanged as if they are equivalent. We must learn to differentiate all the different kinds of work, independently of their concrete characteristics, no matter how different they are. Society reduces work of varying intensity and content to an average, historically variable 'man-hour'. Such an abstract analysis is not without its difficulties. Time is not the only factor which determines the quantity of work and the value attached to it. Marx himself set out the problems of the complexity and intensity of work. In his eyes, work time was not simply to be measured by the clock.

But even if Marxist economists have not tended to lose sight of work as a concrete issue, they have largely tended to reduce it to the important, but limited, questions of pay differentials, time off and external working conditions. The method of relating the work people actually do to an illusory average has been maintained in 'socialist' societies. When any of these comes to count up the workforce at its disposal, they speak of an abstract average, not of the multitudinous individual workers who make it up. What becomes of human beings in all this abstraction? Such economic calculations never get past thinking of human beings as machines. They fail to recognise the living human being acting as a whole person in her/his entirety: in the words of Marx himself, using their brain, hands, muscles, their whole being. In such calculations, rational management of the workforce consists of drawing the maximum physical and mental resources from the employees, whose interests lie in leaving work at the end of the day as intact as possible.

From now to the first decades of the twenty-first century our objectives are clear. We must reduce the average paid working week by 20 to 30 per cent. Inseparably allied to this is the objective of changing the real burden of paid work, and its purpose. In a truly modern society, work must cease to be a curse on the majority of citizens with pleasure only available outside work.

We must not only liberate ourselves from work, but also liberate ourselves within work. These two aims are closely linked. This new, rational approach is ecological in its true sense, because it takes into account in real terms the human (and ecological) costs of work in production and service industries. It calls on us to take to the very limit our fight against all forms of Taylorism.

It also requires us to take into account biological rhythms, above all the fundamental cycle of day and night every twenty-four hours, and to bring back into one global vision all the different aspects that the wage system has separated: time spent directly on work, on the way to and from work, or in training; time spent on activities which are not directly connected to the making of money, whether inside or outside the workplace, and time spent resting. At present, this time represents an important part of the total levy imposed on workers by capital and the state, anxious to maintain control in the periods they do not pay us for.

An enormous increase in the workforce would make it possible to decrease the amount of time each person spends at work. It is important that such an increase should be monitored to ensure that it does not make humans even more subordinate to machines, or increase the destruction of the ecosystem. A reduction in the working week cannot be separated from a change in the ways that we produce and consume, towards ways which use less energy and are less wasteful. Social and environmental European legislation should provide the necessary safeguards.

Society will have to overcome the age-old split between physical and intellectual work, and between deciding and directing on the one hand, and carrying out on the other. The common view of unskilled work as a simple collection of repetitive manual tasks is unacceptable.

The crisis in Taylorism stems from the impossibility of reducing workers to 'operators' who would leave their intelligence and personalities with their coats and expend their energies only in the way strictly defined by their jobs. Computerisation is increasing the mismatch between machines and humans. The substitution of machines and robots for human beings must not be the only aspect of a reduction in working hours. The main motivation should be to promote the role of human beings, their personality and creative autonomy. This means that our priority is to find techniques which are based on work as a living thing. For this to happen, a cultural revolution has to happen in the economy.

Each person, both inside and outside industry, on their own and in association with others, must take control of work processes. The 'world of work' must no longer be a world apart.

A strategy of popular action and initiatives, bringing together disparate groups, could see such a project through. There are a number of problems. A high level of self-management is needed; the project will not succeed if just one prescriptive model is used, nor if we rely on state help. But it does require new rights to be secured and new laws established.

A reduction in working hours must be linked to a raising of low salary levels, and reduced differentials between the highest and the lowest wages. It must be accompanied by a new kind of social and ecological security, community-based and self-managed.

Such a transformation can only be conceived of on a European scale, or at least encompassing most countries in the continent. However, the workers of this continent cannot build 'paradise' on top of 'hell' in the others: Asia, Africa, Latin America and Oceania. The transformation of the working week must be closely linked to the abolition of the neo-colonial international division of labour.

Agriculture

In 1989, over twenty national Italian organisations, including the Communist Party, the Greens, Democrazia Proletaria, the Radical Party, the CGIL, the Lega per l'Ambiente, and Friends of the Earth, put forward the idea of a referendum on the use of chemicals in agriculture. In several European countries new trade union and peasants' organisations sprang up. New forms of agricultural development were experimented with on a local scale.

Agriculture is probably the weakest link in the economic system which controls the planet. Experiments and direct links are possible between peasant farmers in Asia, Africa, Latin America, Oceania and Europe, workers in the food industry, specialists and scientists, health officials, and consumers. Eastern European countries have nothing to lose by helping to solve agricultural problems, which are their economic Achilles' heel.

In Western Europe, the Common Agricultural Policy (CAP), which was put in place in the 1960s, has stimulated a mad race to increase productivity. It favoured the more productive regions, crops and farming methods, and penalised and marginalised the weak. The number of farmers continues to fall. The considerable gap in income continues to grow. The CAP favours agricultural methods which are costly in resources, beneficial to banks and agro-chemical industries, and often harmful to nature and to human health. It has pushed livestock-rearing and arable farming further apart; on the one hand, livestock are kept in factory conditions, are fed chemically processed food and produce toxic slurry; on the other hand there are monocultures without animals, devouring energy and spread with chemical fertiliser.

The EC's policy of farm subsidies has brought about major over-production. Despite quotas and other measures which penalise some farmers, nearly half a billion tonnes of butter, nearly twenty billion tonnes of grain, hundreds of thousands of tonnes of beef, and 250,000 tonnes of olive oil are stockpiled at huge cost in the community's warehouses. This stockpiling is absurd from an economic point of view as well as from an ecological one! The EC has a trade deficit in agricultural products, as it imports animal feed from some Third World countries and the United States. This model of agricultural development contributes to the destruction of forests and land in other continents. The EC strives to export agricultural produce using aggressive marketing techniques barely camouflaged by humanitarian disguises. Competition from cut-price surpluses depresses the world markets, hinders the development of Third World agriculture and makes the peasant economies there even more insecure.

Attempts to reform the CAP as envisaged by governments and EC institutions are based on the logic of liberalism and budgetary considerations. They would lead to the current pattern of agriculture being followed, to land being 'set aside', to more imbalance in how rural areas are used, concentrating production in a few zones and marginalising others (e.g. the Mediterranean and mountainous regions). Such a model is both unjust and fragile. It also provokes resistance, which could lead to a challenging of this agricultural model.

It is high time that we put an end to policies which make the inhabitants of the northern hemisphere over-consume mass-produced food stuffed with chemical residues and synthetic additives, while many people in the southern hemisphere are malnourished and hungry. We must redirect Community funds towards shifting agriculture onto an ecological basis, by moving gradually but resolutely from price subsidies towards policies which favour agricultural employment and incomes without cushioning the richer farmlands, as well as balanced development, technical assistance, and product quality. It is important to give political, economic and social support to all types of organic farming that respect the environment. We must reintegrate agriculture, perhaps with the aid of regional plans, by rationalising the use of pesticides and gradually substituting organic and mineral products for synthetic fertilisers. Research into these areas must be developed in order to provide technical back-up and practical applications for farmers. Small agro-meteorological stations, soil analysis laboratories, and technical assistance or extension services will aid the transition.

Public debate will lead to new standards and legislation, especially to control the agro-chemical and food processing industries. Measures to encourage business and educate the public should concentrate on urban areas and promote demand for quality organic produce. Public institutions – schools, hospitals, and canteens – should be used to pilot projects. A lot depends on the development of producer-consumer co-operatives.

In the middle and long term, the cost of these measures would be amply compensated for by the savings that would be made in the areas of health, water treatment etc. Forests must be integrated into the general context of improving the eco-system with regard to agriculture: reafforestation, no more single crops grown for short-term profit, etc. Such long-term policies pre-suppose that farm and food policy is under the control of society as a whole. The CAP must not be the sole reserve of state apparatus, 'eurocrats' and agricultural industry and financial lobbyists. It must depend above all on agricultural and industrial workers' trade union organisations, associations, and locally elected representatives. Its base will be new social alliances between peasants (who today are scorned, marginalised and evicted from their land) and consumers.

Transformation of agricultural policies in Europe must be thought of as a starting point for other models of development and regulation in the food and agricultural industries throughout the world. For this to happen, markets must be stabilised; prices must be guaranteed for exports from Asia, Africa, Latin America and Oceania; and policies must be put in place to help peasant women and men to increase their productivity while developing their abilities, initiative and organisation.

We are aware that the climatic change which may result from the greenhouse effect may have particularly disastrous results for the agricultural economies of the subtropical zones. We consider that the change in agricultural methods, crops and patterns of consumption which these climatic changes may necessitate should be paid for by the planet as a whole, and above all by the industrialised countries who are primarily responsible for the current greenhouse effect.

The right of all people to food security must be proclaimed and guaranteed as one of the foremost human rights. Any monopoly on globally limited food resources is a way of exerting international pressure and intolerable economic aggression.

Industry, planning and energy

Democracy is not truly democracy if it does not apply to the great economic and technical choices which shape civilisation in the long term. Energy provision, industrial policies and urban growth are of interest to the whole population. In Europe, the great majority of people have always been presented with faits accomplis.

Choice in these matters is the prerogative of groups of technocrats tied to money and power. As a general rule, these groups impose their views by only presenting us with one possibility, instead of a whole range. Meanwhile, scientific developments are increasing the range of possibilities and degree of liberty open to us.

From childhood we are conditioned to respect superlatives: the 'highest' dam, the 'largest' city, the 'tallest' tower, the 'most powerful' power station, the 'fastest' car . . .

In general, the more ambitious a planned development is, the greater its impact on the ecosystem, and the more difficult it is for us to come to terms with all its parameters. New discoveries do not necessarily lead to bigger projects. They allow us to plan on medium- and short-term levels, more than was possible in the past couple of decades.

This is one of the causes of the crisis in Fordism. Large-scale production and centralisation will perhaps remain necessary in some areas. But a reduction of scale and decentralisation will have to become the general aim. Technical refinement is all about developing ways of using as little energy and raw materials as possible, and of caring for people in human, ecological living and working communities.

Pollution and waste are linked, and could often constitute unrecognised and neglected resources. Increased knowledge allows us to systematically put into practice or conduct research into clean techniques, for example by extending the life of products, re-use and recycling. Certain products, such as plutonium and dioxin, must be banned.

At present, policies on work and environmental safety try to control high-risk production sectors by means of standards and protective techniques. The chemical industry is set limits for emissions – prohibitions, and at the same time authorisations, to pollute. The West German hygiene and safety standards cover a hundred thousand pages.

Our change in direction must go further: it must intervene actively and creatively in the heart of the production process. The chemical industry must only produce products which exclude in advance any danger or damage to the atmosphere, water, soil or human life or health. We must question the ways in which chemical products are invented and produced, their social, ecological and economic usefulness. The need is not so much to refine and widen the existing norms for what is currently produced – although this is indeed necessary in most European countries – but to re-think what is produced. In chemistry, for instance, the stress must be on developing harmless products, an ecological chemical industry, and processes for getting rid of the pollution already caused without generating further risks. In the long term, we must try to break our reliance on organochlorine synthetic products.

It is not an ecological system of production which has caused massive unemployment, but its opposite. In our view, a change in direction for industry is intimately linked with a policy of ecological and humane full employment and a reduction in the working week. It is based on the idea of conversion. Industry must have the courage, together with the employees concerned, to face the problems which this will bring – including the forbidding of certain types of production, and factory closures – honestly and democratically.

The expertise needed to make these changes has by and large been accumulated over the years by employees in the industries concerned.

If we do not tackle these problems, nothing will change. As in many of the situations experienced by workers in the past few years, we will not be properly prepared for what ensues, and the results will be all the more momentous.

Military research and production is a large sector where immediate steps towards conversion must be made. Scientists, engineers, technicians, workers, and military personnel from East and West can all join together to achieve this.

We must rethink the use we make of our land: in the cities, where development is linked to the choices we make about production methods, industrialised agriculture, the growth of state apparatus and class inequalities; and in the countryside and the oceans. Alternative modes of transport must be sought. There will be no ecological and humane reorientation without a massive reduction in the use of private motor cars and road transport. It is also madness to increase air transport in Europe.

Any progress towards reorganising society along eco-socialist lines implies a fundamental transformation of energy systems. Some elements of a change in the way energy is used in Europe already exist, for example exchanges of gas and electricity, and linked networks.

The use of nuclear energy in any European country concerns the whole continent, as do the effects of burning fossil fuels. Change on a European scale would make more use of the complementary nature of different reserves of energy, both fossil and renewable, found in the large bio-geographical regions of the continent. It would allow economies to be made on investment, and encourage the perfection of viable scientific and technical energy alternatives. Such a transition would contribute to restoring global balance with regard to the unequal access to energy sources which separates Third World societies from the industrialised societies. It also pre-supposes that the whole European continent will join together to plan a definitive halt to nuclear power, in as short a period as possible. It implies as great a reliance as possible on renewable sources of energy, especially solar energy, to which end a big research programme must be set in motion which should be at least as large as that which was devoted to nuclear power. It is just as important to develop an awareness of energy problems and to reduce energy consumption in all areas: production, transport and buildings. Already in the Western countries, preliminary measures to economise and rationalise usage have proved successful: between 1973 and 1985, energy consumption for all the countries in the OECD rose by 4 per cent, while the gross domestic product rose by 30 per cent.

This success in controlling consumption suggests that the consumers are changing their practices: by renovating existing plants and installing new equipment in others. It calls for the development and manufacture of equipment which will enable us to improve the performance of apparatus which directly consumes or transforms energy (heaters, heat exchangers, engines, light-bulbs, domestic appliances . . .), to develop tools or materials using less energy, and to perfect our energy management. This means that the use of electricity must be strictly limited to specific purposes. It calls for an ongoing dialogue between consumers and producers by means of information and training. A general change in behaviour will be needed. Energy-saving measures in the home, in manufacturing and service industry and in transport will be far more likely than concentrated investments in nuclear or oil programmes to lead to a fundamental, innovative revitalisation of the industrial fabric, to create long-term jobs, and to take a full part in the general change in direction of our lives and production patterns.

All this requires openness, free discussion and self-determination – in short, a practical subversion of the current power structure.

4

Joint action

Social movements will be the driving force behind eco-socialist change. The diversity of their shapes and objectives will disconcert those who see reality through old memories and dogma.

It is sometimes said that all these movements need to converge together. This is a simplistic myth which would not in fact bring about effective change. Concrete alternatives will bring together the majority of the population in a variety of ways: not on the basis of the 'lowest common denominator', but by taking the unique aspects of each social movement as a source of strength and richness. In our opinion, the eco-socialist transition can only entail a plurality of protagonists, of projects and experiments.

Political authorities have difficulty respecting the autonomy of social movements. A new kind of relationship has to be developed. Even the green parties must be careful not to try to 'use' the movement. Eco-socialist change cannot be brought about by the state. So what form of organisation should this alternative politics have? It is this that we now wish to discuss.

Forms of organisation do not solve problems by themselves. But they are one of the stakes in the struggle between, on the one hand, the dominant forces and structures which try to impose their own shape on society; and, on the other hand, currents in the very heart of society which try to liberate us from these constraints.

For centuries the dominant forces have imposed the idea that political awareness is the prerogative of a small number of people: the 'aristocracy', 'élite', or 'avant-garde'. Ever since ancient Greek and Roman times, parties have been devised as male organisations whose aim is to turn the class struggle into a struggle for power.

In the present era, Europe has known two main types of parties: on the dominant side, there are parties of reputable gentry or notables, linked to the establishment; from the dominated side, there are parties of the masses, which involve themselves in other social domains as well as the purely political.

One must be strangely blinkered to believe in today's world that political awareness is the preserve of a minority. Society is becoming more complex, and the political class is disintegrating. The established parties are devoid of solutions. Despite attempts by certain factions to take over or reform them, they are proving powerless to solve basic problems. More and more it is societies themselves, in both East and West, who are tackling these problems despite difficulties, contradictions, and setbacks. In Western democracies, parties become electoral and managerial machines. They organise a significant number of citizens and integrate them into the political system. Beyond the divisions between them, all flounder around in a self-regarding consensus, the main element of which is a metaphysic of the state. All of them, even the smallest groupings, claim to represent the people and to solve problems on their behalf. The party system assumes the right to exercise sovereignty. The return to power of mass parties which organise a whole section of society according to a hierarchy of contradictions is neither desirable, nor, probably, possible. Though not without difficulties, society is taking change into its own hands, in a variety of ways and outside the framework dictated by politics.

We cannot be totally damning, however. Political parties have played a part in informing, awakening and organising the populace. Furthermore, at the current level of theory and practice, the institutions of representative democracy do not appear to be able to function without the aid of competing parties. We do not hide our desire to change the institutions of our countries and of Europe. We hope that centralisation and state control will become exceptions rather than the rule. We place ourselves squarely outside party logic. We only have a future as an alternative force if we can transcend the party system.

We would like to start here and now to try out a different political life, which does not try to ape the established kind. It is a non-authoritarian politics, where the people themselves take direct responsibility for formulating and controlling policy. It is a plurality of contradictions. This radical originality we must bring onto the political scene and into the political institutions.

Working-class history gave birth to trade unions when the time was right; new ways of working together are gestating within the social movements. As eco-socialists we want alternative, independent, green movements to grow in strength, to respond to innovation and to create as yet undiscovered types of political organisations. We therefore hope that the green dynamic does not get suffocated by party politics. Organising as a party is only acceptable as a temporary compromise, in order to keep one's independence and to be able to take part in political institutions. Women must have equal representation. Dissenting views must be expressed and accepted. Responsibilities must be shared, rotated and kept in check. No line, group or person must be able to impose their will over all others; however, individuality must not drown in mediocrity and stereotypes. Parties like this start to make fun of the party system. But old habits and prejudices die hard.

We favour a distinct alternative, and are determining not to form a party, or mini-parties or factions within the green parties. Even if it means being labelled 'eco-naive', we are not fighting for power ourselves. We do not want to be seen as leaders, or as an élite of thinkers. We are but a (necessary) link in the chain. Our aim is for at least some of our ideas to become the fertile ground from which a new society will grow. We would like to be able to take part in actions which lead to concrete alternatives. We do not want to create a monolith. We are in agreement, but there are still differences between us.

We have no fundamental disagreement with the Greens, the workers' movement, or the new social movements. We invite everyone to consider our analyses and suggestions. If thousands of women and men who want a real alternative follow our train of thought long enough to no longer have need of it, then we will have won! By occupying new areas in politics, ecology has proved itself to be independent of statist classification. But there are different currents within it. We have shown that we belong to a current which could be classified as leftist, because of the values we uphold: we want to free humanity from all exploitation and domination, in the tradition of the Enlightenment, the struggles of the workers' movement and the liberation movements in Africa, Asia, Latin America and Oceania, and the women's liberation movement.

We feel that the strategy defined in these pages corresponds to the interests of the great majority of society. We are determined not to neglect anything in order to win it over to eco-socialism. We know that the struggle will be long. As long as our views do not have a political majority, alliances will be necessary in various situations. Even if we do have a majority, alliances will still be needed as different situations emerge. Alliances result from power relationships, but they can also help to change them, and permit us to attain precise objectives of benefit to most of society and to society in general, as well as to maintain or even progress our movement for freedom. The essential thing is that they must never take the place of this movement.

Appendices

Climatic change

By burning fossil fuels, the United States releases 1.3 billion tonnes of carbon into the atmosphere. The Soviet Union and the Eastern European countries emit the same amount, and the EC 0.7 billion.

By the year 2050, the Earth could have become hotter by an average of 2 degrees centigrade – perhaps by as much as 4.5 degrees. This is almost as much of a temperature difference as that which separates the Ice Ages from the warmer periods.

If we do not put a stop to global warming, the map of the world's agriculture will change. The line between forest and prairie – and therefore less rainfall – would move northwards at a speed of 100-150 km every ten years. Production of wheat and maize would be affected, and rice, the staple food of six out of ten human beings, even more so.

At present the sea level is rising by 2mm a year. This is enough to worsen erosion in the deltas of Bangladesh, the Nile, China and the Netherlands. At the end of the next century, the level could have risen by 1 to 2 metres; a catastrophe for the 30 per cent of the world's people who live near sea level.

To count on warming having a beneficial effect on colder regions is scientifically unsound. The Siberian tundra could be reduced to dust. If the great ocean currents change course, northern Europe will suffer.

The majority of humanity would have to make permanent changes in their lifestyle. What price health and survival?

In addition, because of the role of carbon dioxide in photo-synthesis, some vegetable species could disappear, and others would proliferate. These changes would have a knock-on effect on the animal kingdom.

Soil erosion

Less than a quarter of the land on the Earth is cultivable. Of this quarter, scarcely a half (the only really fertile part) has been cultivated for any length of time. The other half is practically unproductive, and could only make a significant contribution to food needs at the price of huge energy subsidies and of an inestimable impact on the environment.

In about sixty countries, desertification is threatening a total area equal to twice that of India. In Africa, an area equivalent in size to Belgium is lost to desert every year.

In many countries the migration of populations away from the countryside is followed by erosion, floods, and landslides. The degradation of the upper reaches of rivers affects the means of survival, the health, and the security of over 400 million people in South-East Asia, and of several tens of millions of people in Africa and Latin America.

The rural exodus and the 'freezing' of agricultural land is not without parallels in Europe. Each year, erosion destroys 16.4 tonnes of earth per hectare in Portugal, and 33.1 tonnes in Spain: countries of which 17 per cent of the surface area is already desert.

At the start of the nineteenth century, less than 10 per cent of the world population lived in towns with more than 5000 inhabitants. Today, two in five people live in towns, and the proportion is growing 25 per cent faster than the total population. In Asia, Africa and Latin America, the large towns are doubling in size every seven years. By the year 2000, there would be 295 cities with more than 1 million inhabitants in the Third World, and 138 in the industrialised countries: the biggest cities in the world would be: Mexico City (over 30 million inhabitants), Calcutta (20), Bombay (19), Seoul (19), Cairo (over 16), and Jakarta (over 16). By that date 50 per cent of the world's population will be concentrated in less than 0.4 per cent of the land area. As towns are always built on the best agricultural land, they are rendering useless one twentieth of the best land. At the same time, they build up noise, fumes, temperature inversions, pollution, water shortages, and mountains of rubbish.

The burden of chemicals that the environment and human beings have to carry is growing dangerously, as much from agriculture as from pharmaceuticals, and from chemicals used in cleaning products, packaging etc. Certain agro-chemicals and intensive mechanised methods used in agriculture destroy humus. The fertility level of the black soil of the Ukraine, formerly a reference point for agronomists, has fallen by half.

Deforestation

In the Erz mountains on the frontier between Czechoslovakia and Germany, the burning of vast quantities of sulphur-rich lignite in power stations has killed hundreds of thousands of hectares of spruce trees. The defoliation extends as far as Lapland. The United Kingdom is as much affected as the most ravaged continental countries by this scourge.

Acid rain is only one factor in this poisoning. Sulphur dioxide from industrial and domestic combustion, and sulphuric acid which is derived from it, can spread over several thousand kilometres. Nitrous oxides, which are emitted principally by internal combustion engines, and their derivative nitric acid, can spread over hundreds of kilometres. Other forms of pollution from cars and agriculture can be added to these. The growth of air transport, 'freed' by the 'wider market', is adding its poisons to the effects of the predominance of road transport.

Even if it is not precisely true that the tropical rain forests are the 'lungs of the planet', it is still true that they form an irreplaceable element of ecological equilibrium. In Malaysia, the destruction of virgin forest has increased by 800 per cent in ten years. Thailand has lost a quarter of its forests in ten years; the Ivory Coast has lost a third in eight years. The forest which used to cover the Indian subcontinent has shrunk by 90 per cent since 1940, and drought is now threatening 1 in 20 of its people. At the present rate, all these forests will have disappeared in less than fifty years. Deforestation adds between 0.4 and 2.5 billion tonnes of carbon to the 5.6 billion tonnes released into the atmosphere every year by the burning of fossil fuels.

Although barely 3 per cent of the area it covers is cultivable, the Amazonian forest is being destroyed at the rate of 40 hectares a minute. Colossal projects envisage the construction of 125 hydroelectric power stations by 2010, with huge dams and artificial lakes which will flood an area of forest larger than Great Britain. Just the Tucurui dam flooded 216,000 hectares of forest. In order to prevent eutrophication, the forest was first sprayed with dioxin (as experimented with by the United States during the Vietnam war). The Grande Carajas mining project, whose cost is estimated at $62 million, would mean the destruction of an area of forest as large as the United Kingdom and France put together.

If land clearances in Indonesia, which are intended to finance the 'Transmigrasi' programme to relocate at least 20 million people, continue, there will be no forest left there in thirty years.

The cleared landscapes resemble photos of Hiroshima. It is estimated that it takes four hundred years for the original elements of a forest to re-establish themselves – that is supposing that the seeds and plants still exist.

Dying rivers and lakes

Without exception, the richer a country, the more water it uses: the United States consumes more than France or West Germany, and these in turn use more than the Italians or the Spaniards, who consume more than the countries of North Africa . . . In France, 17 out of the 37.2 billion cubic metres consumed are used in power stations (both conventional and nuclear), 5.2 by industry, and 4.5 by agriculture. If consumption were at the same level as in the United States, France would need 128 billion cubic metres, or 80 per cent of the flow of all French rivers. Thus, although the Third World is the major victim of water shortages, neither the United States nor the Soviet Union can escape from them. Some regions of Europe also suffer from shortages of drinking water.

In 1965, the zone which delimits a pH level of 5 (which is used to identify acidity in water) could be drawn as a circle with a 200 km radius centred in the North Sea. Today, this circle extends to Singapore. Two million hectares of Scandinavian lakes have reached a level of acidity which is incompatible with certain higher forms of biological reproduction. In the past twenty-five years, agricultural yield per hectare has more than doubled. Hedges and shrubs have been chopped down, ditches filled, ponds and streams have been dried up and roads widened and tarred; such a concentration of development has overwhelmed the countryside, without any thought of the ecological impact.

Indebted farmers succumb to the pressures of competition by pumping water from the ground and destroying wetlands. In the OECD countries 20 million tonnes of fertiliser were used in 1960; today, 50 million tonnes are used on a slightly smaller area. Nitrates are accumulating in ground water, from where they cannot be removed. Levels are rising in West Germany, France, Great Britain and the Netherlands. The water supplies of 700,000 people in Denmark contain over 25 mg/l; for over half of them, the level is over the safety limit of 50 mg/l. World sales of pesticides rose from $3 billion in 1972 to $50 billion today; these will stay in the environment, especially in water, for decades.

Thanks to imported feeds, animals can be farmed in factories at mass-production levels. Most of the nitrogen, phosphate, potassium, plus some heavy metals, that are introduced in the feeds given to these animals, pass into ground or surface water supplies. Ammonia from their dung acidifies the soil. In the Netherlands, where there are 14 million pigs, 95 million chickens and 5 million cattle, these problems have reached crisis levels.

Pollution, dams and dykes, diversions, dredging, land drainage, deforestation of their banks: in numerous industrialised countries, damage to rivers has taken on catastrophic proportions since the 1950s. In the Rhine, one of the rivers that has been the most disrupted for over a hundred years, a large number of eels were recently killed by a spillage of chemicals, serving to remind us that just one industrial crime can wipe out in just a few hours years of efforts to revitalise and repopulate our environment.

At the present rate, two-thirds of the flow of all the rivers on the planet will be controlled by dams. In a large number of these cases, the planners have not taken into account the ecological functioning of these systems. Thus, the Aswan High Dam on the Nile has lowered the amount of sardines caught in the Mediterranean from 15,000 tonnes to 554 tonnes in two years; the floods which used to fertilise an immense band of land along the Nile's banks have disappeared, and thus deprived of silt, Egypt has become the world's largest importer of fertiliser. The groundwater level has changed, and Egypt has therefore actually lost agricultural land instead of gaining more. The result is that Egypt, whose population is growing by one million people every ten months, now imports 40 per cent of its foods; it is being strangled financially; food riots are ensuing.

Poisoned oceans and seas

Oceans and seas cover over 70 per cent of the world.

Most rivers are treated as sewers, and deposit our waste in the seas. Non-biodegradable pollutants such as heavy metals will poison the sea for ever, and will become more concentrated as they move down the food chain. Over two-thirds of the world's population live less than 80km from the sea, and are increasingly congregated in cities. Megalopolis equals megapollution. Around the Mediterranean, three out of four port cities have no sewage treatment plants. Athens, Toulon and Algiers spew their dirty water into the sea. The destruction of the narrow band of fertile sea along the coast kills as much animal and plant life as a forest fire on dry land. Marinas and other developments weaken the coastal zones even further.

Ships flushing out their holds deposit three times as much petroleum into the sea each year as an average oil slick. The colder it gets, the more natural self-purification slows down. The entry of petroleum and other industrial concerns into the Antarctic could be a disaster.

We are constantly being warned: for example, by two million dead sea birds, killed by plastics even in the middle of the Pacific; by the Antarctic penguins with DDT in their tissues, by seals dying on the beaches of the North Sea, by animals smothered with oil, by fish suffocated by proliferating algae.

Population growth

It was in 1840, after about two million years, that the number of human beings reached a billion. Within twelve years, from 1975 to 1987, the human race added as many more individuals as their ancestors did in two million years. There are as many people in (continental) China as there were on the whole planet in Victorian times.

The average age in Algeria is 16.6 years; in Western Germany it is 36.7.

By the end of the century, for one job filled on the northern shores of the Mediterranean, 64 will have to be filled on its southern shores, from Turkey to Morocco.

Unemployment and insecurity in the West

In the EC, the active population (people in or seeking employment) is over 140 million, or 44 per cent of the whole population. This level varies from 37 per cent in Ireland to 56 per cent in Denmark. The service industries provide 60 per cent of available jobs, manufacturing industry a little less than a third, and agriculture scarcely 8 per cent.

Unemployment in the EC has risen from 3.2 per cent of the active population in 1975 to nearly 11 per cent in 1986. These figures only take into account those registered as unemployed.

The level of unemployment has fallen since 1988 in several capitalist countries. But the OECD predicted that in all the countries it covers in Europe and North America put together, there would be 28 million unemployed people by the end of 1990. Contrary to the main trend at the moment, unemployment has risen in Denmark, Iceland, Norway and Turkey.

In the EC, the highest levels of unemployment are found on the northern edges of the community (Ireland, Scotland and northern England), and in the south (Spain and Italian Mezzogiorno). Regions where traditional industry is important suffer from high rates of unemployment.

In the United States, 6000 'restructuring' processes took place in industrial concerns between 1979 and 1986. 91 per cent of these carried out reductions in the workforce and salary cuts as a priority. During this period, the United States lost a million permanent, well-paid jobs in manufacturing industry, while the gross domestic product rose uninterruptedly for seven years. The rise in unemployment was stopped, then reversed from 1982 onwards, but a large proportion of the jobs created were part-time, temporary and badly paid. From 1980 to 1985, the proportion of part-time jobs rose from 10 per cent to 25 per cent of the total. Only a third of the people in such jobs want to work part-time, and 42 per cent of them receive no sickness pay from their employers. In 70 per cent of cases, employers do not contribute to pension funds.

The trend in most capitalist countries is towards badly-paid jobs in service industries. In the United States, Japan, West Germany, France, the United Kingdom and Norway, between 60 per cent and 90 per cent of new jobs in the private sector are created in areas where salary levels are lower than the national average. The only exceptions are Italy, Denmark and Sweden. But Sweden now appears to be heading for an economic downturn.

For the last fifteen years or so, a second job market has been developing alongside stable, remunerative work: the casual or temporary market. For example, in several capitalist countries, the proportion of personnel employed on short-term contracts has risen considerably. Moonlighting and unregistered work are also growing – in fact, all the employment practices which favour exploitation and escape legal controls.

The number of women active in professional work varies greatly from one industrialised country to another. In the EC, 33 per cent of women have a job or say they are looking for one; 39 per cent in Japan; 43 per cent in the United States. The level is much higher than average in Denmark, Great Britain and Portugal, but much lower in Ireland, Spain and Italy.

In all the capitalist countries the proportion of working women (in the narrowest economic sense) rose sharply between 1977 and 1987; in this period of high unemployment, women's determination was such that the proportion of economically active women to the whole population rose by 36 per cent in the United States, 19 per cent in Japan and 18.7 per cent in the EC.

Nevertheless, unemployment affects women more than men everywhere. In the EC at the end of 1988, 8.2 per cent of active men were unemployed, but 13.8 per cent of those women who wished to work – a rise compared to previous years. 52 out of every 100 people looking for work was a woman. This percentage is particularly high in Belgium (61 per cent) and Denmark (54 per cent).

In general, women suffer discrimination in the job market. In the United States, most women employees hold subordinate posts in service industries, and women's wages are on average only 60 per cent as high as men's: no better than in 1955. In the EC, married women occupy 7 out of 10 part-time posts, but only 2 out of 10 full-time posts.

Immigrants are also badly affected by unemployment. In Britain, for the last fifteen years the level of unemployment for people originating from Africa, the West Indies and the Indian sub-continent has been much higher than for white British.

Unemployment hits young people particularly hard. In the EC, on average 17 per cent of people under 25 years old have no job. The level rises to 23 per cent for women.

The majority of young people are confronted by more and more competition in the job market. Unemployment is becoming the fate of many. Their way into employment is increasingly via casual and insecure jobs. Some manage to bypass these difficulties quickly. Many others stay in them for a long time, alternating periods of unemployment, training schemes with no real prospects (except in a few countries), and casual jobs in the informal sector, or short-term temporary work. Some remain there for good, slipping from temporary unemployment to permanent, swelling the ranks of those excluded from prosperity.

Increasingly, unemployment among young people, insecurity and the race for jobs fulfil a kind of selective function for school leavers, in addition to the socio-cultural selective process operated by the education systems in most countries. The children of the most disadvantaged social groups, especially the working class, are excluded from the very beginning.

Deep divisions are thus introduced between workers: between those with a job and those without, between those with stability and those with only insecurity. The young long-term unemployed live more and more on the margins of society; they come to form a world apart; they are socialised into exclusion.

Such insecurity arising from unemployment affects people deeply, even provoking identity crises. In the majority of cases the common factors are inhibitions, disinterest in social life, trade unionism and politics, and conservative backlashes. In 1986, a survey on sexual attitudes was carried out among 20,000 young people in Italy aged 16 to 19. To the question 'What is the problem which arouses the most anxiety and uncertainty in you with regard to the future?', 48 per cent of girls and 46 per cent of boys replied 'a job'; love only scored 4.5 per cent. In the course of a survey on young unemployed people in Great Britain, sociologists noted that 'to talk to them about leisure time was an insult. For many of them, weekends had no real meaning. All days were the same to them'.

Inequality and poverty in the West

There are many gaps in the figures, which make comparisons difficult.

In the foremost capitalist countries, the 10 per cent of households with the highest incomes receive between 30 per cent and 40 per cent of the total income for the whole population; the 10 per cent who own the most property own 50 to 55 per cent of all the property. These disparities are less great in the Scandinavian countries, and greater in the Anglo-Saxon ones.

From figures published by the United States Congress, the average family income of the richest 1 per cent rose from 174,498 dollars a year in 1977 to 303,900 dollars a year in 1988, that is by 74.2 per cent.

In the same period, the income of the poorest 10 per cent fell from 3,528 dollars a year to 3,157 or by 10.5 per cent. As for the middle classes (the 20 per cent who earn from 26,000 to 40,000 dollars a year), their income stayed practically the same. A bad knock for the 'American dream'.

Even these averages are vague, as they compare millions of workers with a small number of people at the top of the scale, whose real incomes are much higher than the average. In France, for example, 10 million salaried workers earn less than £1500 per month (and many of them a lot less than that), while 10,000 people receive 30 to 250 times more – sometimes even 1,000 times more – thanks to their unearned income.

On the whole, financial investments are growing in importance while property and land are losing theirs. In general, the placing and manipulation of financial investments are far more lucrative than work or talent.

Social inequalities are not limited to money. They are increasing in all areas of life: inequality with regard to illness and death, education and culture.

In spite of the development of production and social security systems (which it is difficult to compare from one capitalist country to another), poverty persists – it is even growing, above all among thousands of millions of people in Africa, Asia, Latin America and Oceania, but also in the most industrialised countries, even if its forms are not so acute here.

Various United States governments have tried to fight poverty: at the beginning of the twentieth century, in Roosevelt's time, then under Kennedy. But poverty is still with us, inherent in the structure of society. In New York City alone, 2 out of 5 children are under-nourished; 45 per cent of these are of Hispanic origins, 35 per cent are black; two-thirds of them live in single-parent families.

Poverty is a complex issue. Too many statistical definitions do not grasp its many different aspects. Poverty accumulates injustices: a lack of financial resources, yes, but also lack of a job, poor food, deplorable living conditions, little education, poor health, few social contacts, etc. For many people, poverty is a prison without bars: it excludes them from society.

In Western Europe, poverty affects people in very diverse situations: isolated young people with no jobs, single-parent families (almost all women bringing up one or more children alone), urban, or sometimes, rural, working-class families with many children, the long-term unemployed whose benefit has run out, disabled people, those who are sick for a long period, senior citizens on low pensions (in particular widows); people often topple from insecurity into poverty. Some, of course, do alternate between periods of poverty and moments of being relatively well off.

Using its own definitions, the European Commission estimated in November 1988 that 'in the mid 1970s, there were 38 million people living in conditions of poverty in the 12 states which currently make up the Community. In 1985, according to the same definitions, there were nearly 44 million out of a population of 315 million, or 14 per cent of the total'.

It is undeniable that there are also inequalities in the former eastern bloc states, but it is very difficult to measure the true gap between rich and poor, for lack of information. The poverty which can be observed points to the kind of mis-development which will not be corrected simply by a transfer to capitalist modes of production.

Production and health

The World Health Organisation defines 'health' as 'a state of complete physical, mental and social well-being'. Billions of human beings are far from this state, even in the so-called developed countries.

In Western Europe life expectancy has risen and the great infectious diseases such as tuberculosis have been held in check. One in two cancers are said to be curable. But all these achievements come up against obstacles which are not strictly in the province of either health services or social security.

Life expectancy differs according to social categories. In the last twenty years, it has improved in all social classes, but in the lowest categories (manual workers) it has improved less than in the higher categories (professionals and executives). The gap has therefore grown. In France, for example, 25 per cent of labourers die between the ages of 35 and 60, but only 9 per cent of senior executives and 11 per cent of supervisors.

Such differences reveal inequalities in our general lives and in our culture. They also show the harmful effects of the present system of production, not only on the ecosystems and on consumers, but also (and often first and foremost) on the workers – which are often much more frequent and severe than they think.

There are thus inequalities in life expectancy between workers of a similar level, due to the different types of product and job. Construction workers in shipbuilding or in the aerospace industries can expect to live much longer than metal or foundry workers. The mortality rate among workers in printing works who work at night on rotary presses in a noisy, physically strenuous environment is 10 per cent higher than that of proofreaders and 7 per cent higher than that of compositors.

In most EC countries, accidents at work have been decreasing for several years. However, they are still common (661,000 in France alone in one year). Added to these are traffic accidents. But above all, a large number of technological processes have effects on human beings. Productivism's violence towards human beings at work is compounded by its violence towards the environment and towards all aspects of human life outside the bounds of economically productive work.

Into this category come noise, vibrations, heat and cold, ionising and non-ionising radiation and dust; also, the volume of work and its pace, bad posture, time constraints which lead to physical and mental complaints, fatigue, depression; the innumerable chemical and metallic products such as lead, cadmium, mercury, arsenic, nickel, chromium, tungsten carbide, asbestos, plastic dust, toxic solvents, paints and glues, colourings, lubricating fluids etc. Occupational health care which cuts the patient into separate pieces is still far from tackling the severity of the whole problem. New techniques are continuously engendering new illnesses, for example the effects of VDUs on sight and on the brain.

The ecological state of Eastern Europe

The authorities in the countries of Eastern Europe boasted that they had put into place 'objective conditions' to protect nature better than those in the capitalist countries, as they were influenced neither by the requirement to show a profit, nor by the anarchy of the market place. As evidence they pointed to rigorous laws, some of which date back to the time of Lenin: the abolition of private land ownership and the nationalisation of land (1917), the protection of forests (1918), and the creation of vast reserves (1919). They have displayed the ability to conduct important research, and to put into place concrete measures, which would have enabled, for instance, the Moscow river to be de-polluted, the fisheries of the River Volga and the Sea of Azov to be partially restocked, the air of several large cities to be refreshed using forests as 'lungs', land to be returned to agriculture, and waste water from industry to be recycled.

Perhaps Chernobyl was not directly foreseeable, but a serious accident was probable in one of the most nuclearised countries, simply due to the number of nuclear power stations and their accumulated working hours. The cost of this catastrophe is still impossible to evaluate. Practically every month for the last five years, fresh information has tipped the scales even lower. 79 million people in the Soviet Union received a dose of radiation double that naturally present in the atmosphere. It is foreseen that in the course of the next 50 years, the occurrence of fatal cancers in the Soviet Union will increase by several tens of thousands, perhaps by as many as 200,000; in the rest of the world the rise will be ten times lower, but still noticeable. This is without taking into account unforeseeable genetic mutations in several generations' time. People continue to be evacuated from hundreds of kilometres away. The loss of the power station, the decontamination of the site, the damage caused to people, agriculture, and the surrounding area, could cost as much as £10 billion according to Soviet estimates. Using Western methods of accounting, the financial cost would be much higher.

In twenty years, the Soviet Union and Eastern Europe have doubled their emissions of carbon dioxide. East Germany, Poland and Czechoslovakia have some of the most polluted air in the world. The Solidarity newspaper, which was originally published clandestinely, pours out terrifying information. In five years (1980-85), the concentration of particles in the Warsaw atmosphere increased by 58 per cent. In 1984, in the centre of Krakow, a town whose architectural heritage is considered by UNESCO to be one of the twelve most precious in the world, the concentration of dust (including heavy metal particles) reached 473 tonnes per square kilometre, or over ten times the legal maximum. Every year Czech industry emits 0.2 tonnes of carbon dioxide for each inhabitant. In 1987, Charter 77 distributed a pamphlet entitled 'Let us breathe!' In Hungary, a third of the forests have been irreversibly affected by acid rain. As they accept their responsibilities and verify the facts, the new democratic governments in these countries are discovering the extent of the disaster which is proving to be worse than their worst imaginings.

At the end of 1977, Muscovites discovered black snow for the first time. It had combined with soot in the atmosphere. According to the Minister of Health, the legal limits for atmospheric pollution were greatly exceeded in 104 Soviet cities in 1987. In the course of the last decade, the number of cancers has doubled in the Soviet Union, seemingly because of this pollution. The number of newborn children affected by congenital abnormalities is growing by 5 to 6 per cent each year. This is one of the few countries where – also due to alcoholism – life expectancy is falling!

87 per cent of East German rivers are polluted, and half of those in Czechoslovakia. In Romania, the longest river in the country, the Olt, is polluted for the whole of its length (670 km), except for the first nine kilometres from its source.

In the Soviet Union, the destruction of water sources is reaching terrifying levels.

In 1966, Mikhail Cholokov, winner of the Nobel prize for literature, told the Soviet Communist Party congress: 'I fear that our descendants will never forgive us for having let the sacred Lake Baikal disappear'. In 1986 the academician Trofimuk specified in an official report that at the cellulose manufacturing plant (probably for military use) which ecologists blamed for the damage to the lake, 'for twenty years, the anti-pollution standards have not been respected for a single day'. 50 million roubles' worth of damage had been caused per day, while the factory produced 120 million roubles' worth of cellulose a year! Three-quarters of the lake's 2,500 aquatic species, of which a good number were unique, were wiped out. As large as Belgium, Lake Baikal contains one fiftieth of the world's reserves of fresh water. Its future is still uncertain.

In the Sea of Azov, the fishing catch is nowadays less than 3000 tonnes a year – 100 times less than in 1945.

Within 30 years, the Sea of Aral, the fourth largest lake in the world (120 times larger than Lake Geneva), has gone down by 13 metres, and its level is continuing to fall by 90 centimetres a year. Its surface area has been reduced by 40 per cent and its volume by two-thirds. The uncovered lake floor, which is equivalent in area to Belgium, has turned into a salt desert, where storms throw up millions of tonnes of salt and sand and deposit them on an area of agricultural land covering 100,000 square kilometres. The tripling of the salt level has exterminated 20 of the 24 native species of fish in the lake. In 1957, 54,000 tonnes of fish were caught in the lake; today, none are caught. Summers are becoming hotter and drier, and winters colder and longer. Combined with the threat from chemicals (300 kilos of mineral fertilisers per hectare and not less than 50 kilos of pesticides in the upland region), the salt showers are making irrigation less and less effective, and are threatening the health of 3 million people. The salt is eating away trees and house foundations. Infant mortality has reached 92 per 1000; mothers die young; cancer of the oesophagus is spreading.

The cause of this catastrophe is the 'virgin land' project launched at the beginning of the 1960s. The Moscow government decided to make this region, which straddles the republics of Kazakhstan and Uzbekhistan, produce all the cotton needed in the Soviet Union. As such monoculture needs an awful lot of water, herculean tasks were undertaken to alter the course of two rivers, the Syr-Daria and the Amu-Daria, which flow into the Sea of Aral. Abandoned to the huge level of evaporation prevalent in the region, the giant lake started to empty at an insane rate. The cotton produced is of bad quality. Unemployment in the area is spreading.

In response to the situation, the Ministry of Improvements and Water, Hydroprojekt, decided to divert two or three Siberian rivers which currently flow into the Arctic Sea, by a canal 2500 kilometres long, into the Sea of Aral. In August 1986, the Politburo finally laid to rest this 'project of the century' in view of its incalculable ecological consequences. In ten years, the Sea of Aral will doubtless have halved its size again. It will have become a second Dead Sea.

In contrast to the other industrialised nations, the Soviet Union has built its largest dams on lowland rivers, thus flooding some of its fertile land: 12 million hectares have been turned into lakes or marshes. On the other hand, the drainage of 10 million hectares of northern peat bogs has led to the total destruction of over half of these. The thoughtless clearing of the steppes of Kazakhstan has led to the creation of a 4 million hectares of sandy desert in under 20 years. In total, the amount of cultivable land shrank from 2.92 hectares per inhabitant in 1958 to 2.2 hectares in 1978.

In June 1989, the *Moscow News* published the following table:

	Annual Averages	USSR	USA
Mineral fertiliser used (millions of tonnes of active substances)	1976-1980	18.1	19.8
	1981-1985	22.2	19.3
Pesticides used (millions of tonnes of active substances)	1976-1980	264.0	342.0
	1981-1985	328.0	236.0
Cereal production (millions of tonnes)	1976-1980	205.0	274.0
	1981-1985	180.3	306.6

From 1960 to 1985 the amount of mineral fertilisers used in the Soviet Union increased tenfold, but cereal production only rose from 110 to 1620 kg per hectare. Like Third World countries, the Soviet Union imports chemicals from the United States and other Western countries which are banned in these countries themselves. Details of these purchases, worth $600 million in 1986-87, are a state secret.

The Soviet Union squanders its mineral resources. It extracts five times as much iron from the ground as the United States, using destructive methods. The richest oil deposits are exploited feverishly, with enormous losses. In a certain natural gas extraction plant, which is presented as the height of modern technology, a third of the gas is lost through inefficient methods. Such methods have set off catastrophes such as the earthquake which devastated Nefteyugansk in October 1986. 8 million hectares of reindeer pasture have been destroyed, land polluted, toxic waste buried underground. Corrosion in oil pipelines often leads to accidental spills with no containment system in place.

Governments and businesses in Western Europe are interested in cleaning up the East, which presents an ecological threat to everyone, and also a potential market. The EC is negotiating. An Italian firm has formed a joint Soviet-Italian enterprise with the City of Moscow under the name of 'Prima' to investigate the de-pollution market in the region. At the same time, Western Europe continues to export large quantities of industrial waste to Yugoslavia, Romania, and Eastern Germany in particular. The latter receives 600,000 tonnes of waste from Western Germany alone, mostly produced by the giant chemical concerns Hoechst, Bayer and BASF.

In China and Vietnam, the ecological crises are more like those ravaging the undeveloped countries. During the period of the Chinese 'great leap forward', the growth in the number of smelting furnaces in rural areas, and the priority given to cereal crops, led to the cutting down of a quarter of the country's forests. Since then, droughts have been more frequent, there have been three times as many floods, erosion has been accelerating, the deserts have spread, and reservoirs have silted up. Each year 4000 million tonnes of humus are lost. Due to the lack of purifying plants, 80 per cent of the rivers and lakes are polluted. In 1987, the river Nanzhang beat the word record for the greatest number of people poisoned due to water pollution, with 20,000 people falling ill after a spill from a fertiliser factory.

Glossary

Economism – making best use of scarce resources

Eutrophication – a process by which pollution from such sources as sewage effluent from fertilised fields causes a lake, pond or fen to become over-rich in organic and mineral nutrients so that algae grows rapidly and depletes the oxygen supply.

Fordism/Taylorism – the creation of goods for the mass market. This entails disaggregation of the work process, i.e. specific tasks for specific people to maximise productivity and efficiency. It leads to decline in traditional ethnic radicalism.

Nomenklatura – the expression of an extreme form of state control.

Utilitarianism – a process whereby individuals attempt to maximise utility/satisfaction through consumption: J.S. Mill's hierarchies of desirability. According to the theory, those who had experienced both 'gross' and 'refined' pleasures would always opt for the less basic or gross. The aim of utilitarianism is to escape, as much as possible, from reliance on any source of moral authority.